FISHING FLORIDA IN THE GOLDEN AGE

Tight lines,
Vic Dunaway
Jan 10, 2011

More books by Vic Dunaway:

Complete Book of Baits, Rigs and Tackle

Sport Fish of Florida
Sport Fish of the Gulf of Mexico
Sport Fish of the Atlantic
Sport Fish of the Pacific
Sport Fish of Fresh Water

Angler's Cookbook
Funny Thing About Fishing...

Fishing Florida in the Golden Age

Vic Dunaway

A PICTORIAL MEMOIR

©Copyright 2010 by Vic Dunaway
All Rights Reserved

Cover Design by Dan Dunaway

www.vicdunaway.com

PROLOGUE:

My Alibis

Although it may carry the flavor of both, this book is neither biography nor history. but simply a memoir—the nostalgic recollections and personal photo albums of an old angler whose long life has been driven by the compulsion to fish, and who for more than three-fourths of a century has relentlessly pursued everything from humble panfish in tiny ponds to majestic monsters of the deep sea. Although most of that Fishing has taken place in Florida, numerous other states have been subjected to a share of it, as have dozens of foreign destinations on four continents.

According to the dictionary, a memoir is "a record of events written by a person having intimate knowledge of them and based on personal observation."

Right on the nose, I'd say! The ambition to gain *intimate knowledge* of fishing through *personal observation* has dominated my entire life. Even as a fuzzy-cheeked lad, however, I recognized the cold fact that there were but two possible ways in which I could ever hope to amass the amount of *personal observation* I had in mind, and since I already had failed at inheriting a fortune, I was left with only one way. I decided to become an outdoor writer.

I started reading outdoor magazines at the age of nine and soon began to suspect that people got money for writing those stories. Could that really be true? Yes, it was true! But by the time I discovered that they didn't get *very much* money, or that few of them were able to make their living that way, it was too late to change my stubborn young mind, so I formulated a game plan and stuck to it. I studied journalism in high school and college, and then survived several impatient years of working on newspapers for a paycheck while writing fishing articles on the side. I had just turned 29 when the fates at last gave in and sent me a salaried position as outdoor editor of *The Miami Herald*.

In the half-century that has since flown by I have done no other kind of work, having followed my *Herald* stint with more than 40 years as an editor of *Florida Sportsman* magazine (did I hear a sarcastic comment out there — "*Work?*")

Before I start pouring out memories, I must warn readers that quite a few of the pictures and practices included herein do not stand up to the standards of present-day sportsmanship. I make no excuses. Nearly everybody did it that was back in the "good old days," and nobody's mother ever stepped up to ask, "Well, smarty, would you jump off a cliff if everybody else was doing it?"

During the earlier years of the Golden Age, most fishermen still judged success by the number of fish they were able to kill and bring home. If there was a bag limit, then catching that limit on every trip was their unashamed goal. If there was no legal limit then their aim was to pack their stringers or burlap sacks or ice chests with as many fish as they would hold.

Gamefish that were not considered edible had things only a little better. Many of them were indeed released — ladyfish and jacks with disgust, bonefish and tarpon with pride — and yet many others were killed for no more valid a reason than to snap a picture, enter in a contest, or just hang on a rack as bragging fodder for the triumphant angler of his guide.

But note that Florida's sportsmen—yes, true sportsmen by prevailing standards of their day—once hunted panthers for sport; once included ibises and pelicans among their favored wingshooting targets; once speared leopard rays for adventure.

The standards of sportsmanship evolve with the changing times.

Table of Contents

Chapter 1.....................The Golden Age?, Page 9

Chapter 2.....................Reef and Wreck Fishing, Page 18

Chapter 3.....................Offshore Fishing, Page 36

Chapter 4.....................Nearshore Fishing, Page 63

Chapter 5.....................Freshwater Fishing, Page 108

Chapter 6.....................Points South, Page 133

Chapter 7.....................Boats I have Loved, Page 161

Chapter 8.....................Name Dropping, Page 169

Chapter 9.....................Loads of Lobster, Page 181

THE GOLDEN AGE?

Chapter 1

Considering the fact that Florida has always offered the ultimate angling experience, and continues to do so, the question arises: was there really a Golden Age?

Yes, indeed! There truly was a Golden Age of Florida Fishing. It was a unique period brought about by a set of circumstances that will never again be duplicated.

The Golden Age began after World War II and rolled merrily along for about three decades. Fishing throughout the country basked under that same Midas touch, of course, but Florida wore the golden crown. Florida waters, both salt and fresh, represented El Dorado, the shining dream destination of anglers everywhere. And, as if the state's own angling riches weren't enough, Florida also was the principal gateway to the nearby Bahamas, and to a fast-developing array of sportfishing opportunities throughout Tropical America.

So, why do I nominate that particular time as golden when it's obvious that fish would have been much more plentiful in eras long past--back when Ponce de Leon first showed up in 1513, say? Or even a couple of centuries later, in 1765, when naturalist William Bartram explored Northeast Florida and reported:

"The river, in this place, from shore to shore and perhaps half a mile above and below me, appeared to be one solid bank of fish of various kinds."

The river was the St. Johns, and the fish, though of various kinds, were mostly largemouth bass, which Bartram called trout and which, he said, *"frequently weigh fifteen, twenty, and thirty pounds."*

Bartram was by no means Florida's first fisherman but he obviously was one of the earliest outdoor writers. *"How shall I express myself so as to avoid raising suspicion of my veracity?"* he wondered.

How indeed! But even if we subtract a couple of hundred yards from his mile-long bank of solid fish, and then slice 10 pounds off his estimated weights, we still can't quibble with the assumption that fish were thicker and bigger in Bartram's day.

Nevertheless, the Golden Age of Florida Fishing did not arrive until *my* day. And, thanks to a lucky timing of birth, my own Golden Age happened to coincide with it. Consequently, I was blessed with the opportunity not only to observe and write about that wonderful period from the best seat in the house, so to speak, but to personally wallow in a great many of its previously unimagined angling delights.

Just what kind of alchemy turned that age to gold? What set of circumstances created the magic formula?

Four factors were chiefly responsible:

1. Fish were plentiful and pressure was light. In 1950, the entire population of Florida was slightly less than three million, about the same as that of Miami-Dade County today. Moreover, there was little restriction on the taking of fish. Freshwater bag limits had long been in place but were very lenient, and there were no size limits. Saltwater regulations were close to nil until a 1957 law removed snook from the commercial market and limited anglers to four fish with an 18-inch minimum length. The few other legal minimums were smaller than the average sizes of the species they allegedly protected—12 inches on trout and redfish, for example. There were no closed seasons.

2. **Fishing tackle was being improved and expanded at a revolutionary pace**. The spinning reel took hold in our country in that post-war period and, at the same time, traditional baitcasting and fly reel designs were being refurbished and modernized into instruments strong enough to handle really big fish. Clunky old steel and wood rods gave way to light, strong fiberglass, and later in the Golden Age to graphite and other high-tech materials. Not as obvious but equally important was the evolution of fishing line from natural fibers, such as linen and silk, to rot-proof nylon monofilament and synthetic braids. Every tackle component underwent similar upgrading--lures, hooks, leaders, rod guides, ferrules, accessory gear. All were vastly expanded and improved throughout the Golden Age.

3. **A simultaneous revolution was taking place in the powerboat industry.** Trailer-boating was born in the 1950s and almost immediately touched off a boating boom that in many ways emulated the land boom of the 1920s. Fiberglass was introduced to boat building and rapidly became the hull material of choice. New manufacturers, large and small, began springing up all over the place, as did retail dealerships.

4. **At least equally as important as the other factors there was unaccustomed prosperity**. The post-war period marked the first time that many of our nation's citizens had ever tasted the intoxicating combination of leisure time, disposable income, and available luxuries. For most of their lives they had known nothing but the privations of the Great Depression and the shortages of the Great War. Now, as the Golden Age gathered momentum, many thousands of those citizens rushed to buy the new tackle and fork over down payments on the new boat-motor-trailer rigs. This mushrooming fleet of trailered small

vessels--its weekend skippers armed with ever-improving tackle and navigational aids--proceeded to expand Florida's broad angling horizons as fast as the building of launching ramps would allow. And there seemed to be no limit to the near-virgin territory available.

In Southernmost Florida and the Keys, such romantic-sounding places as Shark River, Lostman's River, the Content Keys, Cosgrove Reef, the Marquesas Keys—to cite only a scant few—had been to the average angler mere fantasy destinations, fishable only by means of extended trips on sleep-aboard vessels. Then, early in the Golden Age, all of those once-remote areas, along with numerous others, opened up to routine day trips and became proving grounds for the many new light-tackle angling specialties that were rapidly being developed or perfected during that post-war period.

Before the big war, adventurous fishermen had found that the tackle and lures they used for freshwater bass also worked very well for snook and small-to-medium tarpon. But that had been just about the extent of light-tackle casting in salt water. Spinning reels were unknown, and although baitcasting and light ocean outfits were common enough along the coasts, they were generally used for trolling, or for drift-fishing and bottom-fishing with natural bait. Canepoles outnumbered rods and reels on many grass flats of the Gulf. On bridges and piers the basic tackle was a handline. Even in deep water the majority of bottom fish, from small grunts to huge grouper, were hauled up by hand. Some partyboats did not even allow rods and reels to be taken aboard.

Not until the Golden Age did sportsmen begin pulling up big grouper, snapper, kingfish and other reef-dwelling prizes with spinning tackle and lines as light as 8-pound test. Not until the Golden Age were baitcasting reels routinely equipped with anti-reverse mechanisms, adjustable drags and spools stout enough to handle the pressures of monofilament line. Not until the Golden Age was the stalking of bonefish in shallow water perfected. Not until the Golden Age were flies deliberately cast at giant tarpon with every hope of a successful outcome.

In the pre-war years of the Great Depression, private fishing boats had largely been limited to displacement-hull cabin cruisers owned by well-to-do sportsmen or charter skippers. Skiff-fishermen, those who could afford them, lugged small outboard motors in their car trunks and clamped them to boats they rented at fish camps for 50 cents or a dollar per day. Ten-horse outboards were the largest in common use, and five-horse kickers predominated.

Out of that slow-poke background arose the postwar power surge, which began with the first mass-marketing of 25-horse engines early in the 1950s and went on to break 100 by the 1960s. After that, the sky was the limit.

The Golden Age tapered off in the 1980s, squelched by such devastating pressures as high-tech and virtually unregulated commercial fishing, irresponsible government tinkering with drainage and wetlands, and rampant urbanization. Adding greatly to those burdens was a vastly increased angling population that had become all too adept at using the sophisticated boats, tackle, and electronic gear that had been spawned in the Golden Age.

Although the period that followed was not exactly a Dark Age, Florida fishing definitely lost much of its sparkle during the late 80s and early 90s, when poor and commercially oriented federal management led to the collapse of at least four major fish stocks--king mackerel, Spanish mackerel, swordfish, and redfish—and the acute depletion of others. Numerous species were in jeopardy at the state level as well.

Happily, angling interests rallied in time to avert total ruin, but it would take years of banging heads against various committees, councils, bureaus, and political bodies to gain significant improvement. Even then, the principal goals, which were to curb commercial fishing excesses and at last put an end to political interference in resource management, would not be substantially reached until well into the decade of the 90s, when voters—after a long and tireless campaign by *Florida Sportsman* magazine and every conservation and sporting organization in the state, overwhelmingly gave their approval to a pair of landmark constitutional amendments. First came the Net Ban, which took effect in 1995. Four years later another amendment merged Florida's splintered and sometimes conflict-ridden management groups into just one, the Florida Fish and Wildlife Conservation Commission, an autonomous agency safe from legislative meddling.

So now, thanks to sound but necessarily restrictive fishery management--along with unceasing vigilance by organized sportsmen and conservation groups--Florida has accomplished an almost miraculous turnaround, and once again holds its accustomed position at the head of the angling world.

But the Golden Age is over. Although a great deal of its glitter still covers every aspect of Florida fishing, the Golden Age, like Camelot, now belongs to history. Unlike Camelot, however, those golden days are verifiable and not long past.

For older sportsman, this book may stir up pleasant memories of their own fishing experiences during the Golden Age.

To the younger crowd all I can say is, "Wow! I wish you coulda been there!"

FISHING THE REEFS

Chapter 2

Back when commercial fishing was limited to hook and line, Florida reefs were healthy and well stocked.

Trophy-size amberjack, snapper and grouper were plentiful. Yellowtail, porgy, grunts, and other "lesser" reef targets were thick in all areas of South Florida and the Keys. Huge runs of king mackerel (more often called kingfish in Florida), were dependable twice-a-year occurrences along both Florida coasts.

Although no surplus vessels had as yet been deliberately put down for the purpose of attracting fish, Florida waters nevertheless held numerous "artificial reefs" in the form of sunken boats and ships, many of them casualties of the recent war. Although some of the Atlantic wrecks lay in waters too deep for easy angling, a number of Gulf wrecks off Key West, the Lower Keys, and the southwest coast were swarming with a huge variety of both bottom dwellers and free-roaming gamefish like barracuda, amberjack, cobia, and permit.

That's a quick picture of the reef and wreck prospects back when private outboard boats were just beginning to proliferate in the Golden Age. Talk about kids getting turned loose in a candy shop!

Early in the Golden Age, quite a few such "kids" began throwing artificial lures on fragile, web-like lines at nearly the entire huge assortment of scaly monsters that hung around Florida reefs. That ridiculous-sounding idea was undoubtedly first conceived by members of the Rod and Reel Club of Miami Beach, the second oldest fishing club in America, whose members had been experimenting with baitcasting and fly tackle in salt water before World War II. The coming of the Golden Age, with its rugged gear and synthetic lines, sparked an explosion of interest in the casting specialties, which now included a third type of light tackle--spinning.

Spinning tackle had long been used in Europe, mainly for the purpose of presenting tiny lures to spooky fish. After the war, it quickly caught on all over America for that very purpose, but in South Florida, Rod and Reel Club members and a few other thrill-seeking anglers had a more daring challenge in mind for the novel gear. Competitors in the Rod and Reel Club's new Spin Casting Division were not shy about throwing lures at anything with fins, no matter how large it might be. They were doing the same, of course, in their Fly Casting and Plug Casting categories.

Maximum line tests were restricted to 8 pounds in Spin Casting, 15 pounds in Plug Casting, and 12 pounds (tippet strength) in Fly Casting. "Plug casting" was a term coined by the club to replace "baitcasting" so as to avoid the implication that natural bait was allowed. Each division carried its own precise set of tackle specifications, but one rule shared by all three divisions was the requirement that only artificial lures could be used, and the lures had to be cast and retrieved manually—not trolled or given action by a moving boat.

The rules might have been confusing to outsiders but they were instantly understandable to members of the Rod and Reel Club, and later to members of various other South Florida fishing clubs that wholeheartedly adopted them and, ultimately, to the general public, which got in on the competitive fun (and frustration) through the Metropolitan Miami Fishing Tournament, whose rules committee and operating membership were composed largely of Rod and Reel Club members. Soon the divisions came to be called, simply, "Spin," "Plug," and "Fly," and it was this widespread emphasis on artificial lures that set South Florida light-tackle anglers apart from all others

When reported in the newspapers, the size and variety of the catches that were being made in all the casting divisions defied public credulity. At the same time, old concepts of "lure fish" kept falling away as competitors continued to hook, and often enough land, many species previously thought to be strictly "bait eaters." These included both large and small reef fish, not excepting even huge grouper. Within a few years, every popular Florida gamefish, along with a raft of lesser known species, had been taken in all the casting categories.

Note, though, that the aforementioned line tests above were not etched in stone. In the mid-1960s, the Met Tournament raised its maximum test in the Spinning Division to 10 pounds, and in later decades all the line tests were subjected to slight juggling by various organizations that conducted tournaments or kept angling records.

Of course, this newfound interest in light tackle did not chase traditional gear off the reefs and wrecks. The masses of bottom fishermen for grouper and snapper clung heavy-handedly to their ocean rods and reels with 40 or 50-pound line—sometimes 80-pound or even wire line if jewfish or other huge grouper were possible catches. Handlines had not disappeared either and, in fact, enjoyed a resurgence after refugees from Fidel Castro took to the reefs wielding their "Cuban yo-yos," which essentially are overgrown spinning reel spools around which the line is wound by hand. In short, every kind of tackle could, and still can, find a happy home on the Florida reefs.

Back in the Golden Age most varieties of reef fish were so much more plentiful than they are today that random deep-jigging could usually be counted on to produce good action. Deep-jigging, of course, was simply vertical jigging carried out in very deep water. Regulation line tests of 8 or 10 pounds for spinning and 15 pounds for plug casting were the norm, but the rods had to be stouter than their freshwater counterparts. No such models were being provided at the time by national tackle firms, so local companies and custom builders had to fill that niche.

Only two baitcasting (plug) reels—the new Abu Ambassadeur and the old Pflueger Supreme—were tough enough to handle ocean fish, and not many spinning reels could meet the challenge. Adventurous spin fishermen had to choose carefully, for the spools of most reels would come apart during the battle with a hefty foe.

Nowadays, the technique of deep jigging is still the same and the system is still deadly, but there is a big difference. Random drifting doesn't cut it anymore.

In the 1960s and into the 1970s not many small-boat anglers even owned a fathometer, much less a loran or GPS receiver. Some club members did have rudimentary sonar—flashers or dials—but the recording units then available were so expensive that they were seldom seen on vessels smaller than sportfishing cruisers or party boats.

None of my own boats ever carried a sounder until after the Golden Age had passed, and yet sons Dan and David and I seldom had to endure a totally fishless day. We used the established random system and, since we usually fished on weekends, we generally could see other jigging boats doing the same thing. The system was simply to motor beyond visible bottom, hopefully to the vicinity of 100 or 120 feet, and then start drifting. The drift normally was northward because of the Gulf Stream, and shoreward because the prevailing winds were from the southeast. We didn't go out, of course, when northers were huffing or when strong southwesterlies foretold a coming front.

Deep-jigging did require some patience, but all the labor was forgotten at the first hookup, which sometimes would come within minutes, and nearly always within an hour. Upon getting a strike, it was vital to throw over a marker immediately. We did not wait to identify the fish, for the drift would have carried us far from the strike-producing spot by the time we landed it. If the catch was a pelagic species — a bonito, say, or blackfin tuna — we would pick up the marker and resume drifting. But if we came up with a grouper or snapper, we would go back and drift past the marker repeatedly.

Deep jigging was the only system that allowed the angler to cover every inch of the water column, and potentially to catch--or at least hook--everything from bottom huggers to ocean roamers.

Rambling the Wrecks

Since the early days of New World exploration, Florida waters have been liberally sprinkled with shipwrecks. While the skimpy remnants of historic wrecks are of little interest to anyone except treasure hunters, ships sunk World War II provided a new kind of riches — a wealth of fabulous fishing. During the Golden Age, a number of those wrecks, located north and west of Key West, became the happy fishing grounds of club anglers, as well as of non-competitive fishermen seeking full coolers. But it took a while for the gold rush to get started.

During the winter-spring "season," there were enough tourists around to keep the boats-for-hire pretty busy, but in the summer and fall, too many unbooked days plagued the charter boats, while the party boats often had to run with only a few fares aboard. In those days, hardly anyone traveled to Key West just to go fishing--not even in high season, much less in summer.

Hoping to ameliorate that sad situation, Jim Sumpter, manager of the Key West Chamber of Commerce, hatched a plan to invite me, as fishing editor of the *Miami Herald*, to his fair city in the summer of 1959, with the aim of exploring areas that the typical charter trips never touched. Sumpter figured I would go nuts over the fabulous fishing, write a stream of enthusiastic columns about it, and, like the pied piper, induce a steady stream of dedicated anglers to follow me to Key West.

I can attest that the first stages of Sumpter's campaign went off exactly as he planned. I came, I caught, and I beat the drums. Eventually, the anticipated stream of new anglers came too, but the flow did not gush at first; it only trickled. Within a couple of years however, it seemed that every fishing club member in Miami was on a permanent commute to Key West.

Capt. Tony Tarracino—later to be Key West's mayor and a saloon-keeper of widespread fame-- introduced me to the wreck fishing, but most of my early Key West wreck rambling was done aboard the sportfishing cruiser *Cay Sal* with Dr. Webster (Doc) Robinson and Capt., Lefty Reagan. In a few years, however, I was wandering around down there in my own trailered boats, or with a buddy.

Although they constituted but a tiny fraction of the endless great fishing water at Key West's doorstep, the Gulf wrecks were the star attractions of the Golden Age, concentrating, as they did, many different kinds of sport and food fish. The best known and hardest-fished of the wrecks were the *Sturtevant, Luckenbach, Gunbor,* and *Bosilka,* but there were numerous smaller wrecks scattered about. In fact, the four biggies named have not been wildly productive in many years. Salvaging operations and natural deterioration had begun reducing the structures even before angling pressure started to mushroom with the development of Loran and GPS.

MY REEF AND WRECKS PHOTO ALBUM

Not many of his fishy opponents were as large as Boog Powell, who at the time of this picture (1970) was the most valuable player in the American League. The foe he's tussling here, however, did have him by at least a few pounds. It was a jewfish in the 350-pound class.

Boog stands aside as Capt. Don Gurgiolo of Islamorada) (with gaff) helps his crew swing Boog's big jewfish aboard.

On the dock of the Ocean Reef Club, North Key Largo, Capt. Bob Lewis (L) and mate Bill Ridgeway display one night's catch of cubera snapper. The two biggest weighed 55 and 52 pounds.

Neither rain nor wind could deter Janey Franklin, wife of my old college pal Harlan Franklin, when she took aim at a big fish. She set light tackle records for kingfish in the 1970s off Stuart—most notably a 43-pounder on 6-pound line.

Here's Janey's big king from the previous photo—not another record but it weighed in the high 30s. Her reel is a Daiwa Silver, one of a series that took the Florida saltwater scene by storm in the mid 1970s.

Al Pflueger Jr., who owned one of the first Formula boats featuring deep-vee hull and center console, introduced me to deep jigging in the early 1960s. Here he pulls on an unseen foe, probably a grouper, off Key Largo.

Deep jigging could, and did, produce strikes at every level of the water column. Here Al gaffs a hefty bonito for John Emery. In the early years of the Golden Age, only a few spinning reels could withstand the pressures exerted by tough ocean fish on monofilament.

John Emery's black grouper was a nice one at around 15 pounds, but certainly no eye-popper among deep-jigging regulars, who caught many lunkers, including an occasional monster of 50 pounds or more, during the Golden Age.

I was out with Al Pflueger when we spotted this weird apparatus off Islamorada in 1963. It turned out to be a longline buoy. We were told that the line it marked supported perhaps 200-300 hooks— elaborate gear in its time. By the 1980s, miles-long lines with thousands of hooks would be deployed off Florida's coasts.

Fish-finding gear wasn't needed back then to catch fish like this nice mutton snapper. Before long, however, Al, who ran a thriving taxidermy business, was to start equipping his boats with the latest thing in recording sonar.

Sons David and Dan ere 8 and 10 when they caught these school kingfish, and a dozen or so more—jigging off Islamorada during a typical fall run.

Dan was a lot happier about his 12-pound cero mackerel than he looks in this picture. He caught it near Alligator Light off Islamorada in 1965. The fish followed his jig from deep water and finally struck under the boat.

Good thing we had no investment in designer fishing clothes. David, age 8, loved hugging his fish and was especially proud of his big red grouper, caught off Key Largo in 1963.

Dan was 13 when he bagged this vividly marked red grouper on one of our main jigging grounds, which was a stretch of close-in blue water south of Careysfort Light off North Key Largo. I always thought that, pound-for-pound (ever hear that one before?) the red was the strongest fighting member of the grouper family.

I weigh in a mutton snapper for Boog Powell at Duck Key while John Emery and Herb Allen look on. The occasion was a one-day tournament in 1975. Yep. Boog won the trophy.

Although it was not uncommon to hook a sailfish while deep-jigging, it was unusual to land one because the heavy jig was so easily thrown during the jumps. That's what happened here, but I chanced to lasso the fish forward of its tail with the flying jig. After that it sounded and died from being pulled backward..

One of my earliest Key West triumphs was a "world record" cobia on fly, taken at the Sturtevant *wreck with Capt. Lefty Reagan on the "Cay Sal". Actually, no world flyrod records were being kept at the time (1960), but this 28-pounder was larger than any listed by the fishing clubs or the Metropolitan Miami Fishing Tournament, and so I shamelessly laid claim to a world record.*

In the same summer of '60, I claimed yet another ersatz flyrod world record with this 31-pound amberjack. Again, it was the largest known to have been caught, but not officially sanctioned anywhere.

This amberjack warily circles a live decoy held at the surface over a Key West wreck. The tactic, later declared ineligible for competitive casting, usually made the curious jacks angry enough to attack an artificial lure or fly.

Even if none of the decoyed amberjack were large enough to interest the competition-driven anglers, they could still be entertaining. Here Jack Rinehart feeds one by hand.

Jim Sumpter of the Key West Chamber of Commerce, spurred me into beating the publicity drums for Key West fishing. The perfect PR man, Jim also caught smaller fish than I did-- this little bonito for example.

*This 12-pound permit was among several I caught one day over the **Sturtevan**t on bucktails. In 1959, permit were considered virtually uncatchable with artificial lures, but eventually it became known that in deep waters they will often hit jigs quite readily.*

Webster "Doc" Robinson, world-famous for his exploits in big-game fishing, was skilled with all forms of light tackle as well. Bob Marvin stands ready to gaff a nice cobia that hit Doc's fly. I sweated this one out, but it was a few pounds lighter than my "world record.

On their way to t Key West fishing spots, small-boat anglers would always pick up a chum from one of the many shrimp boats that anchored during the day. Fishing was often hot, too, around the shrimp boats. The chum did a fine job of attracting trophy fish, but the staggering by-catch of trawling throughout the Gulf would seriously threaten red snapper and other fish stock in coming years.

A club angler bears down with his plug tackle on a cobia that struck over the wreck of the Luckenbach *in 1970. The wrecks were not marked, so before the days or loran and GPS it took heads-up navigation by small-boaters to find them.*

Metallic jigs were all the rage in the 1960s. They worked particularly well on barracuda, and had the added benefit of providing a useful "handle," to aid in landing and releasing. Capt/ Lefty Reagan demonstrates.

With one hand under a gill plate and the other gripping the metallic jig, Lefty released many a 'cuda with no injury to either party. Nearly every one of the droves of barracuda on the Key West wrecks seemed to be at least this big--about 15 pounds -- and some would reach twice that weight, or even more.

This wahoo followed my three-ounce jig up from 150 feet of water off Key West in December, 1966, then struck at the surface. At 34 pounds, it held the Met Tournament Spinning Division record for many years. The skipper was Capt. Reggie Trevor. Staff Photographer Bill Kuenzel of the Herald took the picture.

Only one day after I caught the record wahoo, Dan and I went out with Capt. Bob Lewis on the Miami Herald's sportfishing cruiser RERUN, and Dan, who had turned 13 only a couple of weeks earlier, used the same spinning outfit to jig up a kingfish nearly identical in size to my 34-pound wahoo. I maintained bragging rights, however, as his fish weighed only 31 pounds

Dan's 31-pound king wasn't the biggest fish he hooked that day, just the biggest one he landed. He's shown here on the bow deck of RERUN with Met Master Angler Norm Jansik, battling a pair of monsters that struck their jigs almost simultaneously. Eventually their lines crossed and both fish were cut off.

Al Pflueger tail-hoists a sleek over an Atlantic-side wreck, while fellow Tropical Anglers Club member Dick Coe battles its twin..

Capt. Lefty Reagan and I study the Met yearbook for potential targets on opening day of the 1966-67 tournament. Okay, okay! This was really just a publicity shot.

During his long-hair phase at 14, son David jigged up an 18-pound Almaco jack (L) and a 143 pound mutton snapper from 150 feet of water near Sand Key Light out of Key West.

The next day, at the same bearing off Sand Key Light, David added a fat gag grouper to our mixed bag. In those two jigging trips we landed a total of 11 mutton snapper and, 8 gags, plus an Almaco jack and a blackfin tuna.

With his body attached, this barracuda would easily have topped 50 pounds. Tony Tarracino caught it on a handline with live bait at Fort Jefferson, Dry Tortugas, in 1960. He kept the head for a mount.

Key West had no lock on huge reef fish. Miami waters held plenty of them too, back in the Golden Age. This pair is a 150 pound Warsaw and 90-pound black grouper (also on the gaff at left). They struck on one of Capt. Bob Lewis' many secret deep drops not far offshore of Miami Beach.. David (shown) took turns with Dan and me in cranking up the wire line.

OFFSHORE FISHING

Chapter 3

Offshore fishing shone brightly during the Golden Age, for everything from dolphin and sailfish off mainland shores to giant bluefin tuna in the Bahamas. Both blue and white marlin were at their peak of abundance in the islands and by no means uncommon off Florida coasts. New offshore grounds in the Panhandle opened up early in the Golden age and an entirely new sport--night fishing for broadbill swordfish—waxed and waned before the period ended.

Innovation in big-game reels was not desperately needed. Fin-Nor had introduced its dual-drag, hand-machined (and very expensive) gold series before the war, and those instruments could scarcely be improved upon. Anglers with tighter budgets were not suffering either, thanks to the reliable Penn Senator star-drag reels that also pre-dated world hostilities. Numerous other models made by Penn and Ocean City were entirely satisfactory for a wide range of saltwater demands.

There were still gaps to be filled, however, and in 1966, Penn introduced their gold International series. The first model was the International 50, and the first one of them to reach Florida—so he said, anyway-- was presented to me by Cy Perley, the Penn sales rep. I gawked at it in amazement, realizing that it was going to jump directly into competition with the much higher priced Fin-Nors. The folks at Tycoon/Fin-Nor realized it too, and they shortly responded with a line of their own mid-priced reels, the Regal series. Various other makers introduced new models steadily over the coming years until now, of course, it's easy to find dependable ocean reels in every price niche.

Although reels did not cry out for improvement at the start of the Golden Age, the same could not be said for other components. Offshore anglers benefited greatly in the post-war period from the introduction of solid fiberglass rod blanks that replaced the old split bamboo and hickory shafts. Line guides, reel seats, and rod butts also experienced sharp upgrading, as did most big-game accessories, such as harness and fighting chairs.

The most dramatic advances in offshore angling during the Golden Age came not in tackle but in boats. The lumbering old fishing cruisers of the pre-war era "grew up" during this period. For instance, flying bridges with full controls advanced from being rare add-ons to standard architecture.

Many of the improvements in sportfishing cruisers were spurred by the competitive needs of anglers fishing bluefin tuna tournaments in the Bahamas. The tuna tower, now a common feature on sportfishermen, is a leading example. Introduced in 1953 by Rybovich Boats, the tower not only placed the captain on a high perch for easier spotting of fish but also kept the controls in his hands so he could chase them. Early towers had been little more than crow's nests, from which a spotter yelled instructions to a helmsman stationed below.

Even larger leaps were being made in inboard power, which suddenly expanded in the 1950s from a high of about 150 horsepower to 275 with the introduction of Chrysler's hemi-head V-8. Easier-riding hull designs were coming along at the same time. At long last, offshore boats were becoming capable of traveling long distances at good speeds and in relative comfort.

The same sort of evolution was taking place with smaller, trailerable boats, whose flat hulls—even in otherwise seaworthy craft—usually administered a beating and a drenching to anglers who steered them toward offshore waters. The pounding began to ease up in 1961 with Dick Fisher's introduction of the 15-foot Boston Whaler, the first factory-built center-console boat. It wasn't the console, though, that endeared the Whaler to the public. It was the complex hull design that smoothed out the ride (advertising their boats as unsinkable didn't hurt either). Other designs featuring irregular hulls quickly followed—the cathedral and deep-vee hulls being glowing examples. By the middle of the 1960s, small, open boats were more plentiful on many offshore grounds than charter boats and large inboards.

In addition to the new look in tackle and boats, another landmark change early in the Golden Age had to do with the lines used by offshore anglers. Their strength no longer was designated by "threads" but by "pounds test." The conversion was necessitated by the introduction of monofilament and braids made of synthetic fibers. The old rot-prone linen lines were phased out, along with their old classifications—three-thread., six-thread, nine-thread, etc.--that had denoted relative strength.

Each linen thread had been figured at three pounds of break load. Thus, three-thread line would have tested nine pounds; six-thread, 18 pounds; 9-thread, 27 pounds; 15-thread, 45 pounds; 24-thread, 72 pounds; 39-thread, 117 pounds; and 54-thread, 162 pounds.

Under the new line-test system, these became the 12-, 20-, 30-, 50-, 80-, and 130-pound line classes. The heaviest class--54-thread, 162-pound-test--was dropped.

Kite Fishing Made Easy

In April of 1963 Capt. Bob Lewis called to say he wanted me to see his revolutionary development in ocean angling. It was, he said, an especially deadly tactic for taking sailfish, the pre-eminent targets of Florida bluewater anglers. It involved the presentation of live baits with the aid of a kite.

Revolutionary? Not likely!

Kite fishing already was old hat to Capt. Tommy Gifford, who was chartering his *Stormy Petrel* out of the Ocean Reef Club in North Key Largo. Following Gifford's example, numerous other captains—including Bob Lewis himself-- had become ardent practitioners as well. So— revolutionary?

It turned out that Bob was not exaggerating. Not much, anyway. It wasn't the kite itself, but rather the method and the tools Bob developed, that were destined to make successful sailfish anglers out of many novices who, as the Golden Age waxed bright, were beginning to venture to sea in small boats, often for the first time.

The heart of Bob's new approach was a compact and portable outfit consisting of a collapsible kite in combination with a single-action kite reel on a short and rigid rod. The components could be tucked neatly away aboard nearly any small boat until called to duty. The kite was offered for sale without the reel, but most buyers would choose to include the reel, because it came rigged with the kite line and release clips that made the outfit ready to fish.

After just one action-filled demonstration at the edge of the Gulf Stream, I was convinced that weekend fishermen would thenceforth be able to catch sails and other bluewater fish without ever learning to rig ballyhoo, judge trolling speed, or master the tricky drop-back.

Not all beneficiaries would be small-boat anglers. Skippers of big cruisers welcomed Bob's kites aboard too, simply because they were available. Previously, many captains either had to struggle with making their own kites or else special-order them from custom builders.

That first outing with the kite was only my second fishing trip with Bob Lewis, but --as the reader can't help but notice as he wanders through these pages-- many more were to come. Bob had been a charter captain at Pier 5 for years before taking a private skippering job. Our association was to be interrupted temporarily when he shipped off to England to captain an experimental hovercraft, but after his return from foreign duty, Bob was hired by Pres. Jim Knight to be captain of the *Miami Herald's* charter boat *Rerun.*

As fishing editor of the Herald it was my duty to fish with Bob aboard *Rerun* on many occasions in numerous places, and I must say that I performed my duties loyally and without complaint.

When Giant Tuna Swarmed

Ernest Hemingway landed the first two uninjured giant tuna at Bimini in 1935. They were by no means the first bluefins ever hooked there, but before Hemingway threw his barrel chest, strong arms, and fierce determination into the fray, the tuna (or a marauding shark) had always won—usually at a cost to the angler of a broken chair, harness, rod, reel, or line. And sometimes most, if not all, of the above.

By the time World War II broke out, big things had already happened in the chase for big tuna. Anglers had gained more experienced. Their equipment had improved. Most important of all, the Cat Cay Club had been established and was now up and rolling 16 miles to the south of Bimini. Because the annual schools of tuna came out of the south, Cat Cay was a more strategic location than Bimini, although two or more tournaments were held every year on each island both before and after the war.

In 1939, 44 boats fished the Cat Cay Invitational and racked up 117 giant tuna. In the context of competitive Bahamas tuna fishing, "racked up" can be taken quite literally. All the many hundreds of giant bluefins caught in tournaments before the war and then all during the post-war Golden Age, were killed, weighed—and discarded. Hundreds of others, however, did get released outside of the tournaments.

The glory days of Bahamas tuna fishing began tapering off in the early 1970s, and by 1980 most of the giant bluefins in the Atlantic were gone—done in not by the needless overkill of the tournaments but by commercial longlining and purse-seining. U.S. fisheries management was feeble enough by itself in those days, but tuna management was even worse, having been placed in the hands of a constantly squabbling international commission. Finally, a moratorium was put in place in 1980 and, after that, better controls began to allow bluefins to start growing once more toward "giant" size. A limited fishery now exists in the Western Bahamas, but it is barely dependable enough to attract a scattering of determined individuals. The day of the tournaments is over.

While I was covering the tuna tournaments for the *Miami Herald*, I fished for them a few days myself —at the insistence of Herald president Jim Knight, who assigned his personal boat and crew the task of making sure I did so. Over 10 seasons I managed to survive a dozen on so hookups. I brought two of the behemoths to the scales, released four others, and was fortunate enough to lose the rest of them through blessed mishaps of one sort or another.

Chub Cay — Marlin Paradise

A milestone development in Bahamian big-game fishing was the opening of the Crown Colony Club on Chub Cay early in the 1960s. Chub Cay, southernmost isle the Berry chain, abuts the Tongue of the Ocean and lies on the most-traveled yacht route between South Florida and Nassau. Throughout the sixties it was an angling destination that sometimes rivaled the best white marlin grounds in the world.

Blue marlin were also plentiful in the waters surrounding Chub and many of them were very big. Beyond that, of course, those waters offered the same wondrous assortment of ocean fish and reef species for which the Bahamas are justly famous. It was almost too much that Chub's backwaters were also amply stocked with bonefish.

The Crown Colony Club then was private. Like Cat Cay, it could boast of members whose names were legendary in business and upper social circles, but it was not quite so exclusive. Moreover, its marina facilities were open to transient boats as well as to members, which meant that non-members were able to take advantage of the great fishing in the area.

As president of the Miami Herald, Jim Knight was my boss among many bosses. Jim was a member of the Crown Colony Club, as he was of the Cat Cay Club, and although he was not my direct supervisor, he kept suggesting that I provide a substantial amount of newspaper coverage to the fishing activities at both of those islands, paying particular attention to their numerous big-game tournaments. Recognizing a good suggestion when I heard one, I assured Jim that coverage could be easily arranged.

I was enraptured with Chub Cay and spent far more time there during the sixties than my duties called for. It was great place for family vacations in the summer, and one year Bob Lewis towed my 20-footer over so that I was able to harass all those white marlin on my own for a few days.

It was also at Chub that I fished my one and only big-game tournament. With Bob Lewis at the helm of *Rerun*, I managed to release one blue marlin and one sailfish. I used 20-pound line, which padded the score enough for me to take third place.

The eventual decline of Chub Cay's superb marlin fishing, along with a general decline in the South Atlantic, was due to commercial longlining. Although Atlantic marlins were removed from the commercial market earlier than other major game species, the longliners kept after swordfish for quite some time afterwards. Longlines are not selective. Marlin constituted a considerable by-catch, and even when the marlin were "released" as the law required, they usually ended up dead.

Enter — and Exit — the Swordfish

Florida's most dramatic explosion of big-game in the Golden Age also turned out to be one of the shortest.

Off Miami on the night of July 5, 1976, cousins Jerry and Jesse Webb caught the first two broadbill swordfish ever taken as specific angling targets in Florida waters. Four nights later, another boat reported a catch. Within two weeks, a total of 13 had been taken. Within two years, a rash of highly successful swordfish tournaments had broken out all along the southern coast. Two years after that, the tournaments had folded. In less than five years the great South Florida swordfish bonanza had expired.

But it was fantastic while it lasted. And in that brief span of time, South Florida anglers developed and perfected an entirely new approach to fishing for broadbills. The tools they used and the techniques they worked out would be tried and proven effective in virtually all areas of the world where swordfish waters lay within reach of sportfishing boats.

Was it all for naught? Thank goodness, no. Night swordfishing activity did stay asleep for close to 20 years, but eventually it awakened as fishable numbers of broadbills began returning in the decade of the '90s.

Early federal efforts at swordfish management encountered a huge obstacle. In 1960, the average size of marketed swordfish was over 250 pounds. Two decades later it had fallen to less than 100 pounds, a drop which indicated that most of the big, spawning size fish had already been mopped up by the longliners. The stock that remained was composed mostly of youngsters that had not yet spawned. The feds then put a size limit in place, but it did little good, since most of the hooked fish die before the lines — which span as much as 25 miles — can be retrieved. As already mentioned, those same longlines played havoc with protected blue and white marlin for the same reason: it just doesn't help to release dead fish.

During the period when those original swordfish fireworks were going off in the summer of '76, nobody was luckier at the game than I was. That's a claim I can make even though I didn't catch a single swordfish myself. That's because I never tried. As a writer I was much more interested in observing, photographing and reporting.

When Jerry and Jesse made their historic first catches, I was there looking over their shoulders and taking pictures. I subsequently stowed away with my trusty camera on other boats during those first two wild summers, and got to see swordfish taken every time.

MY OFFSHORE PHOTO ALBUM

Early in my new job with the Miami Herald, I landed this rainbow runner on an offshore casting trip to Cay Sal, Bahamas, with Lefty Reagan and Ted Smits.

I inspect a mixed catch from the deep blue off Cay Sal. The assortment includes rainbow runner, blackfin tuna, dolphin, barracuda, bar jack, and even an ocean tally that somehow got itself hooked on a Mirrolure.

Son Dan insisted for his 8th birthday that we go after a sailfish so I loaded him into our new Boston Whaler and we headed for Islamorada. Here he eyes the bait I planned to drift in the Gulf Stream

Sail on! Was he screaming with excitement or for help? This was the only picture I shot during the epic battle, for I soon was too busy with boat-handling.

Sail in the boat! And it's a first for both the angler and new "captain." Note our sophisticated livewell, which held our one spare bait. A foam ice chest later replaced the bucket as the Whaler's keeper of live bait.

David, in a captain's hat, and Dan, admire this catch of dolphin, always the most dependable targets in our years of offshore angling from small boats. Although seldom as large as these 12-15-pounders, school dolphin were present all summer .On calm days, our fast outboards could cover as much ocean as was required to find them..

Although they didn't necessarily pull any harder, blunt-headed bull dolphin were "neater" than the female "cows," or so thought both my boys. Still David seems as pleased with his cow as Dan with his bull.

In 1965 I got a new toy, the Nikonos 35mm underwater camera. It gave me an excuse to dive into blue water to take shots of hooked fish. The camera's wide angle lens meant I usually had to get very close for a sharp picture.. The dolphin's tail fin (above right) almost brushed my dive mask.

Even with the wide angle, I had to maintain a fair distance to get the full figure of a sail in the frame

This 29-pound dolphin on fly won a writers tournament for me at Islamorada in 1980 — not that winning a writers tournament was any great feat, but it did earn me bragging rights for one evening at the Cheeca Lodge bar.

Dan, center, was also the center of attention, albeit briefly, at the awards ceremony of the 1965 Islamorada Sailfish Tournament. Not only did his three releases in the weekend event win him both the Men's Spinning championship and second-place among juniors, but he received the trophies on his 12th birthday. Ten-year-old David, wearing the "mod" outfit at left, also had a release. We fished the tournament on our 20-foot Scottie Craft, one of two outboard boats in the field.

This sailfish was sorta special. I had caught lots of sails by surface trolling, flatline trolling, flatline drifting, and kite fishing, but this one decided to hit a small piece of cutbait that I was free-lining for yellowtail off Marathon.

Here's a by-catch of my peacock bass trip to Venezuela in 1966 (see Ch. 5). After Bill Morris and I returned from the jungle, we had a day to kill before our flight back to Miami in the evening. Our host, Carlos Galavis, insisted that we fish blue water for half-a-day, and I caught my first blue marlin as a result

On the scale at La Guaira, Venezuela my blue weighed 213 pounds. At that time, the north coast of Venezuela was perhaps the world's top fishing ground for white marlin, but whites were out of season on this trip, so I had to "settle" for a much larger blue.

Harlan Franklin caught his big sailfish at Walkers Cay. It was something of a booby prize, since we were gunning for blue marlin. Walkers, on the northeast side, is one of the Bahamas' top areas for ocean angling. We were fishing a writer's tournament put on by Mako boats. Our vessel was a borrowed 20-foot Mako with a single inboard – great for trolling but a real challenge come docking time

David found it easier to battle his 21-pound blackfin than to lift it afterwards. He caught the tasty tuna on 12-pound trolling tackle during a family outing aboard the Penn Reels company boat out of Sailfish Center, West Palm Beach.

Bob Lewis checks his tackle before our inaugural kite-fishing expedition. As a perk of his private job, his boss allowed him the use of their boat's fancy Fin-Nor gear. This one is a 20-pound outfit

Using a 19-foot wood hull built by Allied Marine in Miami, Bob rigged out a small, open boat solely to promote his kite-fishing kit. He said he put in the livewell first and then added the boat around it. The kite reel (front right) was the metallic prototype of the wooden model he would soon begin selling as part of his kit.

I eventually trained myself to let out the kite line while simultaneously running up the fishing lines, but as Bob shows here, it's a much easier job when two people cooperate.

A live bait suspended from a kite is kept flouncing at the surface, which not only attracts fish from a distance but also makes for a visible strike that can be very near and exciting for anglers in an open boat..

Bob battles one sailfish of a double-header. I stuck my rod in a holder while I took the picture at left, and when I picked it up one five-hundredths of a second later, my own fish was still on. Eventually we released both of them.

Kite fishing produces strikes from all kinds of reef and ocean fish. Here Bob hoists a 40-pound black grouper that took a kite bait off Key Largo and was brought to boat by Jim Salvato. Jim, the father of Joan Wulff (nee Salvato, of course) was an outdoor writer from New Jersey.

The skipper takes his turn as Jesse Webb gaffs an amberjack for Bob Lewis. Note that the kite is still flying on a short leash Bob always harped about how easy it is to keep the kite aloft and out of the way when you kite-fish from an open boat.

In this famous aerial shot by the Bahamas News Bureau, a school of giant bluefin tuna migrates across a sandy bank between Cat Cay and Bimini.

My first giant tuna was a 327-pounder caught in 1963 from Jim Knight's boat. I released two more that same day — having been forced into it by Capt. W.D. Murphy and his Bahamian mate Tony, who would leave no spotted school unchallenged. I'm still surprised that I was able to remain standing long enough for the picture.

The second giant tuna I brought to dock looked twice as big as the 327-pounder I'd weighed a year earlier, and it certainly took twice as long to whip. The scale said 577 pounds.

Jim Knight caught this white marlin on our first crossing together to Chub Cay in the spring of 1963. We put out baits as soon as we hit Northwest Channel, and before we covered the last 16 miles to the marina, we each had released one white out of perhaps a dozen that were raised. Capt. Harold Graves handled the release chores.

Next day I landed a white of my own and then this 224-pound blue marlin. Wow! A white and a blue on the same day! Could there be any greater thrill? As a matter of fact, there could--as I was soon to find out. The three husky gentlemen hauling my blue aboard are, top to bottom, mates Charlie Chase and Chuck Glancy, and Capt. Graves.

Shortly after my blue marlin came aboard, something grabbed our next bait as soon as it hit the water--a mako shark! Since I was on the rod, I was not able to take pictures until a half-hour later, after Capt. Harold Graves sank the flying gaff. Here, Jim Knight is helping him hold the gaff rope.

Even with a second flying gaff in him, the mako is almost a match for three big men — Harold Graves (left), Chuck Glancy, and Jim Knight. Another stalwart was aboard but not available to join the fight. I had to operate the camera.

In the tradition of the sea, we flew "bragging flags" to crow about our unlikely combination of catches. Chuck Glancy had to improvise a mako flag to go with the often-used white marlin and blue marlin pennants.

On the Crown Colony Club dock, my 218-pound mako drew lots of attention. By nightfall that wicked-looking jaw was about the only part left. The rest had been carved into steaks by people from the many boats docked at the marina.

Although tournament champs are sometimes tossed into the drink, also-rans usually escape such treatment; however, my skipper, Capt. Bob Lewis, decided to dunk me after we finished third in one of the last Chub Cay marlin tournaments. As I struggled, Bob stood there laughing, while the two unsympathetic ladies took no notice at all.

In July, 1976 Jerry Webb waits for a swordfish strike, perhaps not patiently, on the Miami charter boat Sea Boots. *Within two hours, the first targeted swordfish catch in Florida history, would have him up and celebrating.*

It's a broadbill! Until the moment it came into view, the thought had been nagging at everyone that this just might be a big shark. Bill Harrison stands ready with the gaff as Steve Fogg handles the leader.

It took all hands to haul Jerry's big broadbill into the cockpit. It would later be weighed in at 348 pounds. But now another question took shape: Was this fish were only an odd interloper or was a new recreational fishery opening up?

Only a few hours after Jerry (L) posed with his monster, Jesse answered the question by nailing another swordfish that scaled within a few pounds of the same weight.

I rode with Anne Kunkel of Palm Beach in the first Miami Sailfish Tournament. Here her crew boats the first of two fish she caught that night

Anne's first swordfish weighed 175 pounds. She added a 145-pounder but still finished out of the money in that wild tourney.

At the tournament weigh-in, Anne poses with her 175-pounder. Scattered on the ground around her is vivid proof that the first swordfish tournament was a rousing success.

On the outing above, Rob Kilgore was the skipper as Don Mann (in tee shirt) caught his first broadbill. Don went on to become the first angler ever to catch every IGFA billfish species in a single year.

Here's another swordfish "first: Al Pflueger Jr. captured a 295-pounder while fishing from his own trailered boat, a 24-foot Formula..

NEARSHORE FISHING

Chapter 4

Skinny water was invented at the beginning of the Golden Age.

Well, it wasn't actually the *water* that was invented; it was the phrase.

Joe Brooks, the most famous outdoor writer of his day, coined the term and popularized it through his many magazine articles. "Skinny water" describes, of course, the extremely shallow flats where anglers stalk bonefish and other game species.

Brooks was the first angler ever to deliberately stalk and catch a bonefish on a fly in skinny water. He did it in 1947, catching two in the same day. It's a fairly safe bet that few, if any, fishermen had successfully stalked bonefish with spinning tackle up to that time either. Almost nobody in America had heard of spinning until 1946, and not until the early 1950s did complete spinning outfits achieve significant distribution throughout the country. A spinning outfit, by the way, was described by another noted writer in 1947 as "a fixed-spool reel, thread line, and extremely light, weighted lures, preferably used with a spinning rod especially designed for the purpose."

Spilling over from pre-war days into the early post-war period, the standard system of bonefishing in 1947 was still not a delicate one. Angler and guide sat in a skiff and waited for the action to come to them. The usual tackle was a light saltwater outfit, and the bait was typically cast out and left for the bonefish to find. Sometimes the angler would not cast until he spotted fish, but the cast had to me made very far ahead because of the heavy sinker required.

Our present sight-fishing system—that of poling or wading in "skinny water" and casting directly toward either the swimming forms or the emergent fins of fish-- was kick-started by Brooks and guide Jimmie Albright when they made those historic catches on fly in '47. Albright told me during our last talk in 1993 (he died in 1998) that neither he nor any of the other early Islamorada guides had ever heard of a bonefish being deliberately taken on a fly before Brooks did it, although several fly fishermen had caught bones unexpectedly while casting to small tarpon or other species.

Anyway, Brooks' catches, combined with the nearly simultaneous appearance of spinning on the South Florida scene, sent Albright and other Keys guides winging off into a brand new era of sight-casting. Using either fly or spinning tackle, anglers now had the ability to cast very light lures or baits straight to the vicinity of the bonefish. Quiet stalking and accurate casting were the keys to this new game, the challenge being to sneak within casting distance and then place the lure close enough to gain attention without spooking the fish. Even baitcasting tackle, modernized in the Golden Age by free-spool reels and fiberglass rods, would soon claim a place in this new sport.

As exploration of skinny water continued to expand in the Florida Keys, so did the types of fish encountered. The first additions were small tarpon and redfish, but then the menu kept increasing until, nowadays, anglers may still get excited when they spot some unexpected gamefish on a favorite flat, but they no longer are surprised.

Bonefish Skiffs Grow Up

When I decided to get my first bonefish boat, more 50 years ago, I was faced with not just a shopping excursion but a voyage of exploration and discovery. I wasn't being picky; there just weren't any such animals on showroom floors. Back then, you could bet that anyone who owned what we now call a flats boat or a bonefish skiff, had rigged it out himself, or had paid a custom shop or independent boatbuilder to do it for him.

Even as late as 1969, when *Florida Sportsman* began publication, you could just about count the factory models on one hand, and maybe have a finger left over to pick up your spinning line.

Nowadays, of course, the angler who plans on shopping for a flats boat faces a daunting challenge. There are literally dozens of different makes, models, sizes, and configurations of open boats designed for high-tech angling and dedicated to the job of getting you into shallow water--and, hopefully, back into deep water again in time to make it home for supper.

But let's go back those 50-plus years.

At a time when the great majority of small fishing boats in Florida were built of plywood or aluminum, I became the proud owner of my first "bonefish skiff"—a 14-foot FiberCraft. The company's name proudly denoted that all its boats were built of that new miracle material called fiberglass (notice I did not say "space-age;" the space age had not yet begun). The designation of "bonefish skiff" was my own. I called it that because it featured a raised forward casting deck as an integral part of its molded cap. Nothing else about the little boat suggested that it was particularly well suited to the fine art of bonefishing. True, it did have an almost flat hull behind a slightly veed bow, but that was the common hull design of the day for outboard boats of all sizes.

To complete my bonefishing package, I added the only two specialized accessories I could think of--a pushpole made from a wooden closet dowel, plus a tubular aluminum extension piece for the motor's handle. That enabled me to stand up and search for pregnant-looking territory while steering the 18-horse Evinrude—a motor, incidentally, that was no small potatoes for its day, since 30 horses were about as many as had yet been corralled under the cowl of any outboard engine

The year was 1958, and the typical 17 and 18-foot skiffs employed by bonefish guides in the Florida Keys didn't really have much more equipment than mine—except, of course, for side-mounted steering wheels and padded seats that gave their clients the expectation of riding in comfort—an expectation that lasted only until the first wind-whipped basin had to be crossed. A fast ride over choppy water in one of those old Keys bonefish boats would rattle your teeth to the roots. By comparison, the ride of my little FiberCraft was not that smooth. When forced to run against a brisk breeze, it not only rattled your teeth but also rearranged most of your internal organs.

Even though I loved as much of that little boat as I could stand, I was deliriously happy, less than two years later, when I got the chance to trade it for a real bonefish skiff—that is, one so named by the factory itself, which again was FiberCraft. Although it was only a foot longer, the new one was wider and (blessedly), built considerably heavier, in order to support a 30-horse kicker, 12 gallons of fuel and integral casting decks forward and aft, with storage compartments underneath. The weight improved the ride quite a bit, even though the hull design was no more sophisticated.

If my increasingly suspect memory is on track, that boat--a cut-down FiberCraft runabout hull with a reworked interior--was the first to be offered by any factory as a specifically designated "bonefish boat." Up to that time, the skiffs used by Keys guides, as already noted, were, either self-rigged or built to order locally.

Several pf the new-generation guides, however, began using the same model FiberCraft that I was attempting to pole--among them Bill Curtis, a local lad who was just building a reputation in Biscayne Bay, and Stu Apte who, although a Miamian like Curtis, chose Little Torch Key in the Lower Keys as his inaugural guiding territory. I fished regularly with both of them—much preferring their FiberCrafts to my FiberCraft, for the obvious reason that their boats were equipped with captains to do the poling and the pointing.

I have talked to anglers over the years who think Curtis was the first bonefish guide to work in Biscayne Bay. Actually, he came along 50 or 60 years too late to be accorded that singular honor, but he may well have been the first to achieve prominence in the Golden Age by stalking his Miami-area bonefish in Florida Keys style. Earlier guides in Biscayne Bay, hampered by heavy boats, generally anchored on the flats, or at the edge of them, and soaked baits on bottom while staying alert for the chance to cast at any passing targets that might be sighted—an honorable system that had long been the backbone of bonefishing everywhere until progressive-minded guides in the Keys seriously refined the sport during the early years of Golden Age.

When you think about it, flats fishing might have gotten its name because early practitioners in the 1920s and '30s used to flat-foot it across inches-deep water trying to throw a hermit crab to a spot where a sighted bonefish might blunder into it. After their feet started getting tired, they figured out that if they fished from an anchored rowboat they could let the bonefish come to them. Eventually, this led to the revelation that if they stood on a thwart they could sight the approaching quarry at a much greater distance. Whether the angler was wading or boating, however, the bonefish was in considerably more danger of getting conked on the head by a one-ounce sinker than of unwittingly gulping down an angler's bait.

Those first seeds of flats fishing were sown in Biscayne Bay shortly before the end of the 19th century, but flats fishing as we think of it today--that is, the picture of an eagle-eyed guide clutching a pushpole in one hand and pointing with the other while his angler unerringly lays out a fly or jig—has evolved almost entirely since the start of the Golden Age--about the same time I started writing fishing stories. I mention this coincidence simply to underline just how brief a time span we're talking about—from my point of view, anyway—and not because I had anything to do with the birth of modern flats fishing.

Something that had *everything* to do with it, however, was the end of World War II, which was followed very shortly by a boom in the development of modern small boats and more powerful outboard motors. The emergence of spinning tackle during the same period also played a vital role, since it allowed the angler to use very light baits and lures and so place his casts much closer to sighted fish. Fly tackle had been around all the time, of course, but only a comparative handful of pre-war anglers had worked up enough nerve to try it in salt water.

"Flats Skiffs" Join the Fray

Up to now, I have mostly been using the term "bonefish skiff," rather than "flats skiff." That's because flats fishing was virtually synonymous in those early days with bonefishing. Even though other varieties of fish were taken with regularity, the skiff-guiding business in the Keys had been built almost entirely on the vast amount of publicity that bonefishing received throughout the country in the late 1940s and the 1950s.

Tarpon, permit and redfish would soon develop a wide flats following as well, but at least a decade would pass before "flats fishing" became a standard term to denote shallow-water sightfishing. As an example, when Bob Hewes Boats came out, late in the 1960s, with what I'm sure was the first boat designed from the hull up for that sort of work, he named it the Bonefisher, and did not even use "flats boat" in his promotional material. Instead, his ads referred to the landmark creation as a "shallow-draft backcountry fishing boat."

Sightfishing for redfish had originally sprung up in the Keys as an offshoot of bonefishing. At some unknown time, bonefishermen started spotting strange black tails among the translucent bonefish tails on certain Florida Bay flats. Exactly when the first Keys guide or angler cast the first bait at a tailing red is lost to history—mainly because the feat was not viewed as anything particularly noteworthy. For years the guides simply took their redfish as they happened to encounter them while bonefishing, but the reds gradually assumed a starring role of their own.

My personal introduction to Keys redfishing took place in 1959 when Capt. Clarence Lowe guided Bill Curtis and me on a long, long trip out of Islamorada to a grassy flat adjacent to Frank Key. We spotted redfish tails and swimming redfish all over the place and caught a bunch of them on bushy Hampson bucktails.

Now, Frank Key was a heck of a long way from Islamorada--it had taken us more than an hour to get there--but my sharply honed angling instinct enabled me to observe that this "distant" flat was located within a long cast or two of the gleaming new motel, marina and boat ramp at Flamingo in the Everglades National Park, and I also knew that many almost identical flats were located in the same neighborhood. That I knew because I had already run aground on most of them while fishing for trout or tarpon out of Flamingo—never realizing that I could have taken advantage of those mishaps to fish for tailing reds!

Clarence and other Keys guides probably weren't too happy when I pointed out in my *Miami Herald* fishing column the proximity of their pet flats to Flamingo. Regardless, it was inevitable that Flamingo—located at the southernmost point of the Florida mainland--would develop during the Golden Age into the headquarters of Florida Bay sightfishing.

During the next couple of decades, the only experience I had (or heard of) in sightfishing for redfish anywhere north of Florida Bay happened in the fall of 1965, when Karl Osborne of Vero Beach invited Al Pflueger Jr. and me to fish a school of big—really big!—redfish that he had discovered on a small and isolated flat just inside Sebastian Inlet. Luckily, the fish were still roaming the flat when Al and I arrived a day or so after Karl's call.

The water was two or three feet deep and the visibility not nearly as good as in Florida Bay, but we had no trouble at all spotting those reds. They kept circling the flat all day long, making humps the size of tugboat wakes as they passed us, and every now and then wallowing in a mass at the surface, thrashing the air with their broad, spotted tails. Each time that happened, our knees turned to jelly. Our casting arms, however, remained functional, which was a good thing, since we needed several hundred casts that day to end up with five fish, all of which weighed 30 pounds or a few ounces more.

Karl checked that flat several times in succeeding years, but after one more good season never found fish on it again.

By the time *Florida Sportsman* arrived on the scene in 1969, redfishing by sight had become a firmly entrenched activity, although it was still confined strictly to Florida Bay, whence it would not stage a full breakout for another

10 years or more. On the other hand, bonefishing was a bigger attraction than ever throughout the Keys and in Biscayne Bay, while interest in shallow-water angling for other species kept mushrooming—especially tarpon, but also permit, shark and, on opportunistic occasions, snook and even mutton snapper.

Two factory boats dominated the flats fishing market during the late sixties and early seventies—the Bonefisher, already mentioned, and the Mako 17, which was not really a "flats hull" by today's definition, but an all-around fishing craft that Mako modified a bit with flats-fishing conveniences. Its higher sides made it more difficult to pole, but many Keys guides liked its roominess, especially for tarpon, and many private anglers chose it because of all-around usefulness. The industry was building momentum during that period, and although numerous boatmakers, large and small, would, as Mako had done with the 17, continue to convert existing models, others slowly began coming out with new and dedicated designs to compete with the Bonefisher.

There were other notable advancements in flats fishing during the Golden Age as well. Basically, shallow sightfishing requires nothing more than a high-floating boat and a stick to push it with. Not much room for improvement, it would seem. Guess again.

First, somebody figured out that a fiberglass pole-vaulting pole would make a lot lighter and tougher pushpole than the old wooden dowel—while providing the angler with a status symbol at the same time. Fancy metal feet—forked for one end of the pole and pointed for the other—soon began replacing the old wooden feet. Then, fiberglass factories jumped in with new pushpole blanks even lighter than the pole-vaulters were using.

So how else can you improve the basic flats-fishing formula? Height, obviously. The poling platform was the next innovation to shake the industry. Its extra height provided far better visibility and, as a bonus, put the poler on the stern and let the angler — at long last — take advantage of that beautiful casting deck at the bow.

Previously, that "casting" deck had mostly served as the guide's poling station. Poling from the stern was more difficult because of weight distribution and because the protruding leg of the hoisted outboard motor kept getting in the way; therefore, most guides would commandeer the bow deck and let his casters work around the motor as best they could. That was no big problem for spin and plug casters, but fly fishermen soon discovered that outboard motors are fitted with at least a dozen line-grabbing protuberances they had never noticed before. The more sympathetic guides might lay a tarpaulin over the motor, but they never offered to swap stations.

I believe that Capt. Bill Curtis, strangely, had the first poling platform. I say "strangely" because Bill was the only guide I fished with who poled from the stern even before the days of the platform. But he loved the added height of course, as did the other anglers and guides who soon joined the fold.

Bob Hewes had a hand in developing the poling platform but at first he declined to put the thing on the Bonefishers he sold. He was concerned about the twin ogres of safety and liability. Platforms look dangerous. In fact, they *are* dangerous. It is no great trick to fall off of one and break something you wouldn't want to do without, even for a while, such as your casting arm. How Hewes and other builders finally resolved their worries about litigation is immaterial, and I don't know anyway, but nowadays it is a rare flats boat indeed that doesn't sport a platform.

By the mid-seventies, toward the end of the Golden Age, flats boats were congregating in considerable number each year on the newfound tarpon grounds of Homosassa, north of Tampa Bay. This marked the first concentrated sight-fishing effort ever to take place outside the Keys or Miami. After that, the many guides and anglers who were by then riding in flats boats began searching for, and often finding, good sightfishing grounds for tarpon in numerous other Gulf Coast areas as well.

Flats fishing for redfish, however, did not really begin to expand northward from Cape Sable until late in the Golden Age. Its roots lay in the appearance of an article in the October, 1981 issue of *Florida Sportsman* entitled "Go Flat Out for Redfish," which explained that reds habitually forage on shallow flats all along both Florida coasts. In that article, I begged readers all over Florida to look for reds in their own backyards.

"Next to nobody outside of extreme South Florida fishes for reds on the flats," the feature noted, adding that "many an undisputed expert in Central or North Florida will flatly tell you that in a lifetime of redfishing he has never even seen one up there on foot-deep flats. And he's telling the truth. He has never seen them there because he has never been in such skinny water to look for them. The great majority of fishermen in most areas of Florida avoid that kind of water like the plague."

While neither that article nor the continuing boom in flats boats caused any immediate gold rush to the redfish flats of Central and North Florida, it did stir up keen interest in exploration. Over the next several months, enthusiastic and sometimes incredulous, reports of success kept trickling into our editorial offices from far-flung areas outside South Florida, including the Indian River, Charlotte Harbor, Tampa Bay and the Big Bend. Flats fishing had begun to build a head of steam in every sector of both Florida coasts.

And finally, around 1990, everything seemed to peak at the same time: Flats boats had become numerous and available in various prices. Even more importantly, redfish were once again swarming the flats up and down both coasts of Florida, following their removal from commercial exploitation in 1988.

Snook and trout soon joined the list of popular species fished by sight in the back country, even though both species were more often caught by casting into potholes, muds, or channels.

And, of course, permit and big tarpon eventually became more coveted prizes than bonefish. Permit were ready eaters of crab baits and even live shrimp but they were tough to fool with artificials, so the great challenge in permit fishing was to entice strikes with flies and jigs. Tarpon, on the other hand, would strike lures greedily— when in the mood to do so; therefore the challenge in tarpon fishing was to land bigger and bigger specimens on light casting tackle.

In the late forties and early fifties, huge tarpon were being landed on baitcasting gear in the hands of skilled anglers guided by pros such as Albright, but fly fishing for really big tarpon was largely considered an exercise in futility until after 1955, when the "legalization" of heavy tippets in competitive angling, along with the introduction of Fin-Nor's gutsy machined fly reel, at last made it feasible to attack giant tarpon with fly tackle. That challenge has been a dominating specialty ever since.

Giant tarpon cannot navigate in water quite so skinny as can bonefish and reds, but they often cruise atop clear but deeper flats and along edges that are shallow enough to allow both easy sighting and effective casting with floating fly lines.

More Fishing Grounds

Meanwhile, at the start of the Golden age, such mainland bays as Lake Worth in Palm Bach County and Biscayne Bay in Miami-Dade, were blessed with vast annual runs of Spanish mackerel, often accompanied by substantial numbers of bluefish and pompano. The Indian River and its many offshoots, along with bays, canals and other waterways farther south, held snook, redfish and tarpon, along with husky mangrove snapper, trout and numerous other popular species. Good fishing from shorelines, bridges and piers could easily be reached in most areas.

But there was sad news too, in the form of dredge-and-fill operations that began after the war in Miami's North Biscayne Bay and in Lake Worth, Palm Beach County. Fishing in both those areas was adversely impacted for years by the siltation that resulted when post-war developers rushed to create valuable waterfront land out of what formerly had been rich breeding grounds for fish. Eventually, the state would put an end to indiscriminate dredging, but it would take decades for the bay bottoms of South Florida to fully recover.

Fortunately, South Biscayne Bay—below the Rickenbacker Causeway and Key Biscayne-- was largely spared from the dredging and so, like the Florida Keys, South Bay remained a varied and fertile area, not only for migrating mackerel and blues, but for many resident sub-tropical species including bonefish, permit, and tarpon.

And Across the State

Before Florida removed snook from the marketplace in 1957, quite a few "recreational" anglers used to fish for them commercially along the Tamiami Trail in Collier County. The gear that many employed was a flyrod. I often wondered if those commercial fly fishermen looked down their noses at people who sold snook caught on less prestigious tackle.

Fishing for snook in canals along the Trail is still practiced today, sometimes with noteworthy success, but drainage projects and residential developments have long since made that fishery a hollow echo of what it was in the Golden Age. If snook were suddenly declared a market species once again--Heaven forbid--I'm afraid commercial flyrodders would now starve to death.

Everglades National Park was established in 1947, just as the Golden Age began to yawn and scratch, but not until 10 years later did the Flamingo visitor center, with its marina and launching ramp, open for business at the southern tip of the Florida mainland. In its pre-park days, Flamingo had been a commercial fishing village, reachable by land only via a miserable road that scarcely deserved the name. Once that road was paved, eager anglers could travel from Florida City to Flamingo in less than an hour, and many of them already had trailer boats to tow behind them. Over the next 20 or 30 years, I was to make that drive far too many times to count.

Flamingo's strategic fishing location was immediately apparent. Out front (to the south), Florida Bay and its many little isles stretched over the horizon to the Florida Keys. Out back, a string of interconnected bays--Whitewater Bay being the largest—extended all the way northward to storied Shark River. To the west and north of Flamingo, on the Gulf shore, lay Cape Sable with its three sandy (and fishy) points called East Cape, Middle Cape and Northwest Cape.

As trailered boats gained speed and range, some of them occasionally continued north from Shark River to Lostman's River, and there perhaps met other small-boaters who had ventured equally far south, picking their way through the intricate and then-unmarked waterways of the Ten Thousand Islands.

Some 20 miles north of Everglades City was Marco Island. It was mostly sand and sandspurs when I joined the Miami Herald in 1958, although it did boast villages -- Marco and Caxambas—at either end, and they were connected by a paved road.

A motorist wishing to leave that road and head for Marco Beach did so at his peril. I got stuck several times but, like many other exploration-minded anglers of that period, I carried a shovel in the car trunk. I never had much trouble digging out of the sand, and the effort was well worthwhile--not only for the snook, redfish and trout that cavorted in the surf, but also for the diverse and colorful seashells that kept my young family occupied during our all-day outings from Miami.

Outside of my usual South Florida stomping grounds numerous other fishy Gulf destinations were always beckoning in the Golden Age. Boca Grande Pass, on Gasparilla Island at the mouth of Charlotte Harbor, was prominent among them but certainly not alone. On various occasions over many years I was privileged to sample the near-shore riches along the full length of both Florida coasts--and also in the Bahamas, which I considered just part of my home territory.

As for Boca Grande, a great many Florida anglers might picture a Golden Age as one in which its innumerable tarpon were seldom annoyed by boats or baits.

And when might that have been? At the time of the Tequesta Indians?

How about the 1960s, and even the 1970s?

Sure, even in those days the place was jammed with eager tarpon-seekers from all over the country, but the big crowds were there only during the short "season" of May and June. After the last spring tide in June, most visitors departed for cooler climes and Boca Grande pulled in its shutters. The few motels and restaurants that remained open sliced their prices to the bone, and for the rest of the summer the tarpon enjoyed a great deal of hassle-free time.

I always tried to schedule my trips to Boca Grande in July, when traffic on the water was predictably minimal and often nearly non-existent. The local charter boats continued to stay fairly busy, mostly during alternate weeks, when they fished in the early morning and again in the evening on each day of spring tides, but those boats adhered to the time-honored and productive habit of drifting in a pack over an unvarying course. Visiting cabin boats, whether private or charter, usually just joined the pack and went along with the established routine. Visiting trailer boats sometimes drifted with the fleet as well, but most of the small-boaters who went to Boca Grande that time of year were there to take advantage of seasonal rates, and to catch up on their fishing for snook—or redfish, or grouper, or trout, or maybe even the tripletail that hung around many of the channel markers in Charlotte Harbor.

You'd never know it if you kept your eyes only on that tiny section of the pass favored by the fleet, but tarpon were everywhere. You could cruise the entire pass, as well as the Gulf waters that bordered it, and spot pods of rolling fish. After a little trial and error, I discovered early in the seventies that by motoring upcurrent of rolling tarpon, I could then drift back through their area while working a jig gently near the bottom and hook a fish nearly every time. They were all big—probably 70 pounds at a minimum—and so I was just as happy when they threw the jig, which they usually did.

Not many old hands back then believed my assertion that Boca Grande's supposedly picky tarpon were suckers for jigs. The guides mostly used live crabs or squirrel fish (sand perch), which they drifted deep with the help of breakaway sinkers.

Today, jigs are among the standard offerings.

MY NEARSHORE PHOTO ALBUM

Joe Brooks (L) and Capt. Jimmie Albright pose with some early bonefish taken on flies by sight-fishing. I got this picture from Jimmie during my last talk with him in 1993.

A retired Capt. Jimmie Albright is surrounded in his Islamorada home by memorabilia of his long career. I took this picture five years before his death.

I'm chatting here with Joe Brooks (the handsome one on the left) just before a trip in 1958. We did not sight-fish in Joe's famous "skinny water" but instead jigged for tarpon in the Key West ship channel. Joe was living in Islamorada at the time.

Capt. George Hommell Jr. of Islamorada was the first bonefish guide I ever fished with, and he was to become one of my most valued friends and mentors over the years. We were often together, both in Florida and on foreign trips. After I left the **Miami Herald** *in 1968, I became a consultant for* **World Wide Sportsman,** *which he co-founded.*

Gar Wood Jr. (R) was the son of the famous 1920s auto and speedboat racer Gar Wood, but he was better known in South Florida circles as the designer of the pioneering Fin-Nor fly reel, as well as other high-quality fishing reels. Here, he and I are chatting at a Met Tournament awards ceremony in 1965.

These two early prototypes of the fly reel designed by Wood and machined by him out of solid aluminum bar stock were owned by Capt. Jimmie Albright.

My No. 3 Fin-Nor (reel No. 40) has been through the wars since I first got it in 1960. The loss of its gloss is due more to rough weather and bouncing boats than to the punishment meted out to it by the many and varied fish it has taken.

I wore this hat hoping Capt. George Hommell would mistake me for an experienced Keys angler, but it only gave me away as just another outdoor writer. Nevertheless, George patiently guided me to this fish, and a few more, on our first outing.

Is that a tarpon? I don't think so! But this 35-pound kingfish was my only catch on a tarpon-fishing trip to Bahia Honda with Dave Meyer, manager of the Tycoon/Fin-Nor Company. The year was 1958.

Harry Gilbert, a good pal and an owner of Gilbert's Fish Camp at Jewfish Creek, lived in my South Dade neighborhood. Launching at Gilbert's camp, I fished areas as far-flung as Flamingo to the west, and offshore Key Largo to the east. And many great spots in between.

Things happened so fast early in the Golden Age, that the "firsts" weren't easy to pin down. I do believe, though, that Capt. Bill Curtis — framed above by his landing net-- was the first bonefish guide to practice skinny-water poling in Miami's Biscayne Bay. His fisherman is J. Lee Cuddy, a widely-known Miami tackle supplier and top all-around angler.

My good pal Al Pflueger Jr. fights a bonefish in the proper style. The high rod position keeps much of the line off the water, out of the way of mangrove shoots or other obstructions. Al and I conducted a traveling seminar on fishing during the early 1970s.

Lefty Kreh arrived in 1965 to take over for the deceased George Robey as manager of the Met Tournament. Lefty was dying to catch a permit, and who better to find him one, I figured, than Curtis? Here, Lefty leads his prize toward Curtis' waiting net

A hooray for Lefty Kreh's first permit! Over the next, say, half-a-century or so there would be many more to come for both Lefty and Capt. Bill Curtis.

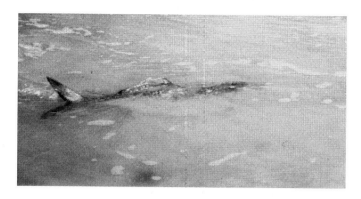

The sight of big tarpon cruising the edges of shallow banks in Florida Bay touched off a flurry of fly-fishing in the mid-1950s, when the use of a heavy tippet at the end of a fly leader was first approved by the Rod and Reel Club and the Met Tournament. Anglers began tossing their flies at these huge fish with renewed vigor, and records began to fall.

Capt. Stu Apte was yanked overboard twice before he finally gaffed the record tarpon at left for Joe Brooks in May of 1961. It weighed 148.5 pounds and stood for 10 years before it was finally broken, at 155 pound, by Joe's erstwhile guide, Stu Apte himself.

Capt. Russ Grey found this non-record-size tarpon, liberally estimated to weigh 15 pounds, for my 12-year-old son Dan in a creek near Big Pine Key in1965.

Tarpon of all sizes could be hooked, and some of the smaller ones landed, from many Keys bridges by night. At left, Ed Louys helps Celie Chaplin show off her catch, which was destined to decorate an office wall of the motel owned and operated by the Chaplins in Marathon.

In 1961, Dan and David, then 8 and 6, went sight-fishing with me for the first time. Capt. Ralph Knowles guided us out of Islamorada and we returned with a haul of redfish from the flats and trout from potholes. Dan caught several sighted reds and David got one, although not the one he threw his jig at.

Over the years I caught two sawfish on sight-fishing flats in Florida Bay. This was the bigger of the pair and it got released. The smaller one — about half this size — still hangs on my wall. Sawfish now are fully protected.

George Robey, manager of the Met Tournament when I arrived in Miami, hefts the nice shook he caught in a Florida Bay finger channel. Capt. Al Lipford guided.

Lefty Kreh, shown unhooking a Florida Bay redfish, was hired as Met Tournament manager after the sudden death of George Robey in 1965. Although I'd lost a treasured friend, Lefty took his place as a new pal and frequent fishing buddy. The Met was wholly funded by the **Herald** *in those days, so I was naturally a close ally of the manager.*

Somewhere in that mini-jungle there is water and, Dan hopes, an infant tarpon waiting to smash his tiny plug.

"Right back atcha pal!" That's what the juvenile tarpon might be saying after jumping and flinging Dan's plug.

This is what the trouble was all about? Anyway, I suppose we thought it was great fun at the time.

I was a witness in 1969 when Herb Allen, my longtime pal from Tampa Bay, caught this big permit at Key West. It was so heavy I volunteered to hold his rod for him.

Ten years after he caught his first Florida Bay redfish by sight-casting at a different fish, son David, now 16, took this one near that same flat. And this time it was the one he aimed at! During the 10-year interim he had accomplished the same feat lots of times.

A colorful character in Everglades City during the 1950s and '60s was Rocky Weinstein, said to have once been a minor mafia figure. He was widely recognized as the Papa fly fisherman on the Tamiami Trail. Other anglers, including Joe Brooks and Ted Williams, flocked to him for advice. He later got a boat and became a backcountry guide.

Rocky often guided me to good snook fishing, with an occasional bass thrown in. The lure at the end of my rod is a wooden Creek Chub Yellow Darter, which was the No. 1 choice for snook on the "inside," meaning the 10,000 Islands backcountry.

I "discovered" Cape Sable's Middle Cape beach in 1960, during an outing in my new 15-foot Whaler. Ed Louys shows one of several big snook we caught while walking the beach that day. Neither of us knew of the now-famous spot beforehand, but there was no mistaking its fishy look. Middle Cape is about 20 miles from Flamingo in the Everglades National Park

This kind of picture often resulted when outdoor writers hit good action in the 1960s. That day we caught many more trout and reds than are shown here, and also several more snook, but Ed Louys wanted this variety shot for his article in Salt Water Sportsman. *In that day and time, tarpon were often sacrificed (blush!) merely for photos.*

Dan Schooler and I camped out with our four lads on Middle Cape Beach one weekend in 1963. Mugging at right are (L-R) Tim Schooler, Dan, David, and Pat Schooler.

The boys were thrilled by Schooler's 15-pound snook. It was, the only one, we caught that weekend. Trout, however, were plentiful and hungry.

When a marauding blacktip shark kept stealing our hooked trout at Middle Cape Beach I rigged up a heavy outfit and caught the robber. The boys got revenge by pelting it with seashells.

Here's another fishy beach – isolated Marco Beach – near Naples, north of the National park. In the background is Bob Whittaker, manager of a resort at Marco village, which at the time was the island's most densely populated community. My colleague Jim Martenhoff took these pictures for the Miami Herald. *We often caught nice snook from Marco Beach but with a deadline to meet we were lucky to get a couple of small ones.*

When I took this picture of the old Goodland bridge in 1990, I seemed to recall that it wasn't in much worse shape 20 years earlier, when it had been the only way to reach Marco Island by road – usually after waiting for the bridge tender to crank open a swingaway section by hand for a passing boat, and then crank it closed again.

A State News Bureau publicity excursion to Lostman's River in 1959 produced this famous (well, it used to be famous!) publicity shot of me waging battle with a 25-pound snook. Funny how the fish maintained that same picturesque pose throughout the long photo session! For a number of years afterwards this picture seemed to pop up everywhere,- from billboards and postcards to place mats and sugar packets.

Six-year-old David flashes a grin almost as big as his first snook, which he caught in the mouth of Little Sable Creek between Cape Sable and Shark River. The mackerel was so unexpected that Danny decided to toast it with a swig of Coke That big outboard motor was the most coveted seat on our Thunderbird and the scene of many a territorial battle between the boys.

One fall day in 1964, the family was dunking fiddler crabs for sheepshead from the dock at Marco Island Inn. Dan was outfishing all of us by about 2-1. At first I thought he had found some new technique, but finally decided that his tee-shirt with the sheepshead stripes was the secret.

The pipe and the old straw hat were props for this publicity photo of me taken by the Florida State News Bureau in 1962

Although he also welcomed redfish, Capt. Andy McLean, was the leading "outside" snook guide of his day in the Chokoloskee area. "Outside" meant the shorelines, oyster bars and passes along the edge of the Gulf. "Inside" referred to the mangrove hinterlands of the 10,000 Islands.

Andy McLean nets a big snook for Henry Orr, while Lefty Kreh works for another. Andy gave me my earliest lessons in coaxing strikes from deep-hanging snook by easing a bucktail slowly along the bottom.

Hank Orr, who founded the Spinmaster Rod Company, caught this no-spot redfish and "normal" one-spotter with Andy McLean. Spinmaster was one of the best-selling fiberglass rod lines in Florida during the 1960s and '70s.

David nets a nice snook for Dan on Andy McLean's **Snook Dust II in 1966.** It was caught on a trolled spoon. The boys preferred casting to trolling, but catches like this had them agreeing that Capt. Andy always knew best.

I fished with Andy once or twice a season for more than two decades. By the time I caught this beauty with him in he late 1970s, he had downsized from a cabin cruiser to a Hewe's Bonefisher

Dan compares Spanish mackerel with Boog Powell offshore of Cape Sable in the winter of 1972. It was a tie so we went into extra innings. Boog really didn't need to travel that far to get mackerel. He lived in Miami and spent many of his off-season days fishing for mackerel in South Biscayne Bay.

Dan Schooler nailed his 12-pound redfish at the mouth of Shark River, in 1970. A school of the big reds kept parading back and forth along that shoreline in the background and we managed to catch three of them about this same size.

The beach at Middle Cape Sable had its share of ups and downs over the 40 years or so I fished it, but when it was good there was no more enjoyable spot. Here, Dan is trying to unhook one snook while watching his pal Jim Caple tussle another in 1971.

Speaking of downs, how about these castaways? We were marooned on Northwest Cape in 1970 when my brand-new 115-horse motor conked out. Nelson Bryant of the New York Times *prepares planked trout for our supper while I try for more in the surf. Lefty Kreh is busy taking the picture. We got a tow back to Flamingo next day.*

Dan Schooler fishes for jewfish in Shark River, using a Calcutta pole and a live mangrove snapper for bait. This kind of fishing was fairly common at the time, circa 1972. Other folks in the boat are its owner, Jesse Webb, and Bob Lewis.

Here's the 100-pound jewfish Schooler finally caught after it yanked him and his pole from bow to transom. Bob Lewis saved him from going overboard by grabbing his belt.

Bob gaffs the big fish and Jesse passes him a rope to string it on. This fishing isn't legally done anymore, not even for Goliath grouper, which the jewfish is now called by the politically correct.

Norm Jansik took this world-record, 242-pound jewfish on 12-pound line at Flamingo in 1969. A freak catch? Yes and no. Competitive anglers worked out a system by which they could hook such monsters under a navigation marker, then manage to keep their lines intact until the quarry fled to open water, where a long fight could then be successfully concluded. See next picture for an explanation.

Flip Pallot demonstrates how he and some of his peers were able to catch giant jewfish on very light lines in the late sixties and early seventies. They climbed from the boat onto the marker, hooked the fish on a live bait, and then kept passing the rod from hand to hand around the pilings to protect the line. If all went well, the jewfish would eventually leave its haven and the angler's pal would pick him up.

In 1969, Helen Robinson needed a catch on 130-pound line to complete a sweep of world records in every category. Slightly built and in her seventies, Helen could not climb up onto Marker 2 so she gamely hung on to her rod until Capt. John Scudder backed clear. Her record weighed 372 pounds.

The young permit held by my son-in-law Johnnie Patronis was one of a variety of fish we caught from a Florida Bay channel near Flamingo during his visit in 1979. We also caught trout, redfish, snook, and black drum.

A "tailing flat" near Flamingo turned up this husky redfish in 1980 for Karl Wickstrom, founder of Florida Sportsman *magazine, who fed it a weedless Johnson spoon.*

Although Flip Pallot could find giant tarpon in Florida Bay as well as any guide, he also knew where their babies liked to hang out. Flip (R) located this little beauty for fly fisherman Rex Gerlach, a Daiwa exec, in the fall of 1978.

Janey Franklin casts to a redfish off St. George Island in the Panhandle in 1968. Other hunting dogs may point birds, but the several dachshunds that Janey and husband Harlan have owned always pointed fish.

A well-barked struggle is about to come to a happy end.

Not be outdone by wife and dog, Harlan also collects a nice red from the same beach-running school.

One of the first redfish taken by sight-casting anywhere north of Florida Bay was this 35-pounder caught by Al Pflueger Jr. on a flat just inside Sebastian Inlet in 1965. Karl Osborne of Vero Beach, a freelance writer and Al's taxidermy agent, had spotted the school of big reds a few days earlier. They were still there when Karl led us to the place but he doubted they would hit. He was almost right.

It took most of a day and a few hundred casts on that Sebastian flat to get five reluctant strikes, but Al Pflueger and I luckily landed all five of the fish, which weighed between 30 and 35 pounds. Al took one of his three reds on a fly. The others all hit swimming Mirrolures. Karl Osborne (R) helps me pose with them. All the fish were mounted for Pflueger Taxidermy displays.

What's so strange about the above shot of rolling tarpon in Boca Grande Pass? Give up? Well, there isn't a single boat to be seen on a sunny summer afternoon in July, 1970. Although plenty of tarpon still remained in the pass, the island virtually went to sleep after the May-June "season".

I connected with lots of big tarpon on jigs at Boca Grande in the late sixties and early seventies. The battle I'm concluding here took more than 30 minutes, during which time the fish jumped only twice – once soon after it felt the hook, and again just after being released (R).

In 1975 Al Pflueger Jr. and I conducted a fishing seminar in Daytona Beach. As a perk we were escorted to Ponce Inlet to cast for the big (by Florida standards) bluefish that frequented the jetties. Al, clad all in white, is casting a surface plug.

The bluefish in Ponce Inlet were no suckers, but we got a few by working close against the rocks — the closer the better. This one weighed 8 pounds.

Jesse Webb, one of the swordfish pioneers from the preceding chapter, retired and moved to Stuart. Karl Wickstrom and I helped him catch a few school bluefish like this one near the St. Lucie Inlet in the early eighties

In 1957 I got an assignment to write about whiting in the surf, so my wife and I fished the beach at Canaveral to get pictures. Every whiting we caught was scrawny but Cheryl's pose in her stylish clam-diggers, or whatever they are, carried the story.

Dan was six in 1959 when he caught a 47-pound cobia at a marker off Marco. We'd spent more than an hour trying to fish up a bait, but only kept catching and throwing back catfish. Finally I caught a snapper, which the cobia eagerly gobbled. Upon cleaning the catch, I was shocked to find its belly full of catfish in various stages of digestion.

One summer weekend in 1964, the kids were away on a visit to their grandparents, so Cheryl took the boys' usual place in our Whaler and caught this snook near Jewfish Creek.

FRESH WATER

Chapter 5

For about three decades following World War II, Florida was the Bass Capital of the World. If you were around back then you would have seen support for that claim on signs and billboards all over the state. What difference did it make if various chambers of commerce claimed that title specifically for their own local lakes and rivers? The whole was the sum of its parts, and the whole was Florida, the dream destination of bass fishermen all over the country.

Nobody doubted that Florida waters held the biggest bass in all the land. Yes, it was true that the world record was held by a Georgia fish at 22 pounds, 4 ounces, but that bass was an obvious freak of nature, an inexplicable aberration. Florida was the *real* home of the lunkers, and the reason was as plain as the nose on my face, which is very plain indeed: our state was the owner of its own proprietary sub-species—*Micropterus salmoides floridanus*, the King Kong of largemouth basses. Local legends of 25- and 30-pounders abounded, and many localities could actually show you proof of 18- or 20-pounders that had been taken from their backyard waters.

In the eyes of most bass fisherman of that period, however, the potential for an occasional giant catch was not nearly as attractive as finding consistently good action on bass of all sizes, including many lunkers. With a few exceptions, Florida's lakes and rivers were healthy and productive during the Golden Age. Limit strings were common, but I will not allow nostalgia to suggest that empty strings were unheard of. Golden Age or not, there never were and never will be any guarantees in fishing.

In those days, the bag limit for largemouth bass was 10 in most of Florida, although in a couple of places it was 15. Anglers had no minimum or maximum size limits to keep track of. As for bream (the collective Florida name for all species of freshwater panfish except crappie) the limit of 50 per person was the same as it is today, but the only rationale for a limit was to deter commercializing.

Many biologists firmly believed that no amount of hook-and-line fishing could ever threaten the welfare of warm-water fisheries, and that the only reason for imposing any bag limits on bass was to increase angler satisfaction by allowing folks to brag about their limit catches. The scientists weren't necessarily wrong; it's just that such conclusions pre-suppose a balanced biomass in a healthy environment — conditions that became increasingly rare in Florida as the years fled by and big agriculture and development flourished.

These day, if you should happen to be planning a swing around Florida to try different bass-fishing lakes you'd better check with an attorney first. Maybe together you can plot the different bag limits along your projected itinerary — 10? Five? Less than five? The limits are assigned geographically, with local exceptions, and only a couple of lakes in the whole state allow 10 bass per day.

And that's the easy part. Keeping track of the size limits might require not only a lawyer but also a mathematician, in order to plot the variations in minimum size, maximum size, and slot sizes.

Lake Okeechobee is Florida's biggest and best-known bass lake, and historically the most productive. So let's use "the Big O" as an example. Anglers there may keep five bass, provided each is less than 13 inches or more than 18 inches in length. Read that carefully. Ordinarily, the "keeper" slot is *between* such a set of figures, not above and below it.

The point of all this is not to ridicule Florida's freshwater fish management, but to praise it. Complicated times call for complicated action. Most of our inland waters now carry immense burdens, created by such constant pressures as poor drainage practices, agricultural and urban runoff, and, of course, an ever-mushrooming population. In addition, bass fishing is no longer just the pleasant though often exciting pastime it was back in the Golden Age. Now it largely is a highly structured and often competitive angling activity that targets big fish. Consequently, Florida biologists were compelled to restructure their management in the early 1990s, switching from the previous goal of (a) producing the most fish for the most people to (b) fostering a larger percentage of trophy fish to please the modern hordes of regimented largemouth bass fishermen.

I should have had a premonition of the looming "revolution" in bass fishing when Roland Martin called me up in the late fall of 1967. I had met Roland a short while earlier in South Carolina, where he was guiding on the Santee-Cooper lakes. Now he was in Miami on a road tour with Ray Scott, a fellow who had recently established an organization he had cleverly named the Bass Anglers Sportsmen Society (B.A.S.S). Roland was a star of the society's early tournaments and was stumping with Ray to help him sell memberships by putting on seminars. I plugged their event in the *Miami Herald*, and attended it myself, along with maybe two dozen other South Florida bass fishermen.

Then, after a post-seminar chat with Ray and Roland, I put the struggling new group out of my mind and went back to having lots of fun catching lots of bass in Lake Okeechobee and the Everglades.

But I was going to hear much more about B.A.S.S. in the near future.

And in the far future, of course, B.A.S.S. was to be taken over by ESPN and plastered all over weekend television.

The Million-Acre Playground

Some called it an engineering marvel, while others called it an ecological disaster. Both observations were absolutely correct.

But there was also a third view of the three vast water-storage pools that had been created during the 1950s as a joint project of the Central and Southern Florida Flood Control District (FCD) and the Army Corps of Engineers. The FCD issued a pamphlet calling it "The Million Acre Playground" and for the next decade or so few freshwater fishermen would pick fault with that description. Even today, most of the facilities and fishing opportunities encompassed by the Everglades Water Conservation Areas remain in place, but the bass fishing, although still very good at times, has declined a great deal from the days when it was not uncommon for parties to release 100 small bass per trip, while also picking up a lunker or three along the way.

The Everglades Conservation Areas comprise a system of canals, levees, spillways and pumping stations that sprawl across the majority of the Everglades between Lake Okeechobee and the southern Gulf Coast.

The three "Pools" are dubbed Areas 1, 2 and 3, and back in the day they were conversationally referred to as Loxahatchee, Sawgrass, and Holiday Park—those being the names of the recreational concessions that had been granted in each area. The FCD (whose name was later changed to the South Florida Water Management District) also provided a liberal array of non-commercial facilities throughout all the areas—ramps, picnic tables, and virtually endless bank-fishing for non-boaters.

Each of the pools was basically a huge lake surrounded by canals. During high water, flooded marshes in their centers could turn out some spectacular catches of big bass for anglers willing to wade or pole their boats through the pads and reeds. High water also brought fast fishing for bass and panfish below spillways and flood gates.

And at times when flood turned to severe drought, some of the canals would get so jammed up with fish that the Game and Fresh Water Fish Commission would suspend bag limits and encourage fishermen to take out as many of the overcrowded bream and bass as possible.

There is not room in this little piece to even begin outlining the devastation that "water management" has visited on the historic sheet flow in the Everglades, or the peril in which it has at times placed the Everglades National Park and Lake Okeechobee. Books and articles on the subject are legion, and new articles are being written nearly every day. Here I will comment only on the factors involved in the gradual erosion of fishing quality throughout the region.

To begin with, a natural decline was inevitable. The Everglades Conservation Areas, after all, were simply new impoundments, and all new impoundments generally experience an explosion of great fishing for a few years before settling into normality. Add to that the degradation caused by nutrient runoff from the adjacent agricultural areas (Big Sugar and big truck farming), along with crippling drought-flood cycles, and an intrusion of exotic species, headed by the oscar cichlid. The oscar, in fact, became the dominant species in many of the canals.

Sure, cichlids may be easy to catch and pretty good to eat, but the one-time abundance of fat largemouth bass and native panfish is sorely missed by all who were privileged to wet their lines in the Conservation Areas during the Golden Age.

When the Peacock Became a Bass

Late in the 1950s, American sportsmen began hearing reports of a spectacular but little-known gamefish that lurked in South America's Amazon and Orinoco watersheds. Called *tucunare* in Brazil and *pavon* in Spanish-speaking countries, this fish was said to be as aggressive as a barracuda and as beautiful as a--well, as a peacock, which is what *pavon* means in English.

Interest in the *pavon* ran especially high in Florida after the Game and Fresh Water Fish Commission began a study in 1963 that was aimed at determining the suitability of this much-ballyhooed fish for introduction into Florida waters. To make the peacock sound even more appealing to bass-crazy Americans, somebody got the inspired idea of tacking "bass" to the end of its name. And so was born the "peacock bass," which it is not a bass at all, but the largest member of the cichlid family.

In that distant time, no commercial angling facilities existed in any of the *pavon's* native countries. Anyone with a yen to fish for this near-fabulous species would either have to become an intrepid adventurer like the early Amazon explorers, or else connect somehow with a local sportsman who was willing to act as host and guide. In the spring of 1965 I made just such a connection through and with Miamian Bill Morris, a former resident of Venezuela and a businessman who still had many important contacts in that country.

One of Bill's contacts, a good friend named Carlos Galavis, sounded especially important—not because he was a high government official but because his family owned a ranch in the heart of Venezuela's *pavon* country. Carlos offered to fly us there from Caracas in his private plane and help us "investigate" the sporting qualifications of the fish that was presumably to become a new addition to Florida's angling menu. Carlos himself, of course, had no need to investigate, for he had spent a large portion of his youth working and playing on that ranch, and he knew the fishing intimately.

Meanwhile, back in Florida, the peacock bass project went sailing along under an ever-increasing air of optimism until a freeze in February of 1966 unexpectedly killed every fish in the experimental ponds at Miami Lakes, thus crushing the three-year-old experiment.

Happily, however, the story does not end there. Twenty years later, like the Phoenix rising from its ashes, the peacock bass project sprang to life once more. And this time the fish was not viewed simply as an additional gamefish, but as a biological control to help curb the hordes of smaller exotic species that had taken over in so many South Florida canals and waterways during the intervening years.

The old research from the 1960s proved to be of great value as the Commission worked through various problems and pitfalls. Eventually it was determined that Florida's southernmost canals are deep enough to protect the fish from any freeze that might occur. And so in July of 1989, a full quarter-century after the idea first took root, the peacock bass finally gained a spot in the hallowed lineup of major Florida sports fish.

My Fresh Water Photo Album

Dan and David, at the tender ages of 7 and 5, caught their first limits of fish by walking the banks of Government Cut at the north end of Lake Okeechobee. At left David adds another speckled perch to an eventual total of 75 (I caught my limit too).

On several occasions in the early sixties, morning duck shoots out of Camp Okee-Simmee ended quickly, but that enabled me to trade gun for rod and go wading for bass. The ducks in this photo are a three-man limit of 12, but I caught the limit string of 10-bass all by myself.

Many memorable days of wading over grassy shallows in the big lake produced limits of 10 bass per angler, with some in the 4- to-6-pound range. On especially memorable days, a couple of 8- or 9-pounders might be included. Butch Reutebuch shows how we did it.

These bass, seven to nine pounds, were gleaned from three stringers. The other contributing anglers were Wells Kelley and guide Butch Reutebuch.

Roadside canals and bayous in Florida are sometimes as fishy as they look. I found this three-pound bass off SR 60 in Polk County in 1963. What was I doing there? I was on my way to Lake Kissimmee to go bass fishing, of course.

Mark Challancin managed the J-Mark Fish Camp near Belle Glade in the southeast corner of Lake Okeechobee. Strings of bass like the one he's holding were pretty common everywhere along the south and west shores of the lake.

Lake Okeechobee seemed to lead the world in 9-pound bass and yet 10-pounders were rare. Any one of these three that I caught in one morning out of J-Mark Camp would have been my personal record from the lake. Two weighed 9.5 pounds and the other 9.75 pounds.

117

Guide Harold DeTar of Moore Haven (R above) organized an annual fly fishing tournament during the prime bedding season for Lake Okeechobee's abundant bluegill and shellcracker. His "bream tournament," as it was generally called (even though bass counted in the scoring) generated business and publicity for the lake in the slow summertime. Some of the canal settings were picturesque (below).

When Alligator Alley opened in 1969, we didn't travel it all the way from Fort Lauderdale to Naples. We were just pleased that it took us to some fast-paced fishing for bream and small bass in many canals and culverts. Much later "The Alley" became a segment of I-75.

Dan stands on a flooded culvert to cast his fly into a canal in the Big Cypress area traversed by Alligator Alley. At times, nearly every toss around a culvert resulted in a strike from a bluegill or juvenile bass.

Lefty Kreh's son Larry helped us collect this string of bass from a newly dug canal in the north end of Everglades National Park in 1969

Dan's string of bass came from a spot in South Dade County that we fondly, if itchily, called the "redbug canal." We fished it over a period of six or seven years and seldom failed to get both bass and chigger bites.

A writers' meeting in Sanford in 1977 provided the excuse to drift Beetle Spins in Lake Monroe for speckled perch. Since our sons were not present, Cheryl had to take over their usual role of catching more fish than I did.

A favorite spot near our South Dade home was this rockpit near Homestead Air Force Base, where Dan is fly-casting. Although the biggest bass always came from the county's many rockpits, we preferred action on smaller fish to live-baiting for lunkers.

Speaking of lunkers, one cold morning in 1970 I fished Lake Jackson near Tallahassee and brought back these two eight-pound bass. I figured I would be the hero of the day until I returned to Red and Sam's Camp to discover that another angler had weighed in a 15-pounder-- nearly as big as my pair put together. Back then Lake Jackson was the nation's glory hole for giant bass.

By the middle of the 1970s, Cheryl and I had raised our own private guide. David had moved to Cross Creek and his business card read "Over 10 Guide Service." Above, he nets a big one for his mother at Newnan's Lake. And, yes, it was definitely over 10 (below), weighing a shade under 12 pounds. It still holds the family record.

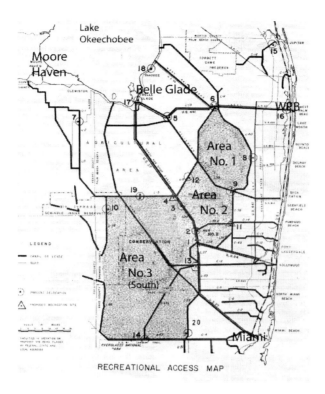

The three Conservation Areas blanket most of the territory lying west of Florida's coastal megalopolis and east of the major agricultural area. Golden-Age anglers generally joined other conservation voices in protest of environmentally damaging practices but nevertheless took full advantage of great fishing in the canals and water-storage pools.

Meet the oscar. Now dominant in many Everglades waterways, the existence of this exotic species was unknown to the general public until I caught one in South Dade in 1958 and announced my "discovery" in the paper.

On our first trip to Loxahatchee Recreation Camp, which served Area 1, we enjoyed the expertise of a guide whom I remember only as Johnny. Here he displays the bass we caught that day in 1962.

The first big bass of Dan's 11-year life was the 6-pounder he's lifting here in Area 1. The picture can't do justice to the suspenseful struggle that had just taken place in a tangled battleground of weeds and pads

Dan displays his prize catch and the Rapala balsa plug that lured it out of its weedy hideaway. This was in 1964, three years after our first trip to Loxahatchee Recreation Camp in Conservation Area 1.

Within just a few trips of Dan's 6-pounder, David also bagged a big one. His 4-pounder was two pounds lighter, but seeing as how he was two years younger than his brother, it seemed fitting. This fish struck a spoon at one of the spillways on the rim canal west of the Loxahatchee Recreation Area camp.

The scene shifts to the interior marsh out of Everglades Holiday Park in Conservation Area 3. It's 1967, and 13-year-old Dan is re-enacting the climactic scene of my epic battle with an 8-pound largemouth.

Although we could have had no premonition at the time, this shot of Dan admiring the 8-pounder was to become the cover shot on the first issue of Florida Sportsman *when the magazine debuted a couple of years later in 1969.*

125

The photos on these two pages were taken in 1965 during a period of severe drought that dried up the interior marsh and crowded the fish into the canals. The action took place along the Tamiami Trail (U.S. 41), which forms the southern boundary of Conservation Area No. 3.

David adds a bream to our long stringer. We walked this stretch of canal on several occasions during that drought-parched summer, each time bringing out at least a full stringer of bream and another of bass — all caught with topwater plugs and flyrod bugs. Bag limits had been suspended so we indulged ourselves by catching fish until we dropped, then making presents of them to pole-fishermen, who caught far fewer than we did because they stayed glued to one spot.

Friend Kevin Wendland helps David hoist a stringer of big bream. Strangely, we caught few bass on the No. 6 flyrod bugs we were using. Even though the bass were mostly 12-inchers, they much preferred the bigger meals offered by our three-inch Rapala plugs.

Kevin's work is never done. Now he's called upon to help Dan display a string of bass. There was no point in casting close to the edge, so we seldom lost a lure. Both bass and bream were roaming and feeding freely all over the canal.

This is a different stringer of bass — honest!-- but it was caught on the same day. On our first trip during the drought we caught and counted over 100 each bream and bass. On succeeding trips we never bothered to count. After several weeks, the strikes finally did taper off so I guess we helped make at least a minor dent in the overcrowding.

In times of stable water levels, we often fished the several dams along the Tamiami Trail. David caught this little bass from Conservation Area 3 on the north side of the highway. Everglades National Park lies across the road on the south side. These dams interrupted the flow of fresh water into the Park and were eventually removed.

Closer to Miami, the Tamiami Trail was narrower so the WMD created several parking and picnic areas where people could fish away from traffic. But, sadly, they were far less productive than the wide-open stretches of highway several miles farther west.

We fished on occasion at Mack's Camp near the intersection of SR 997 and U.S. 27. Back then, all the canals in that sector were newly dug and teeming with young bass.

Biologist Vern Ogilvie headed Florida's original peacock project in the 1960s. Here he's using non-clinical gear to test the reactions of the fish he was raising in several Miami Lakes ponds. The project finally failed when a rare hard freeze hit South Florida in February, 1966 and killed every one of the fish.

Tom McBroom, then chairman of the Game and Fresh Water Fish Commission, was the leading supporter of the peacock as a new Florida gamefish. He was always happy to help by fishing up some of them for re-stocking into additional grow-out ponds.

Three generations of peacocks (R) swam the Miami Lakes ponds when the freeze hit. As it turned out, the Miami Lakes fish would never have been stocked anyway, even if the experiment had been successful. There are several different species of peacocks in South America, and Ogilvie later learned that this one, which had come from Iquitos, Peru, was a smaller, desirable type.

Under the watchful eye of Bill Morris and an unidentified canine observer, Carlos Galavis unloads gear from his Cessna Skymaster. Carlos flew Bill and me from Caracas to his family ranch in the llanos (flatlands) of Venezuela, our headquarters for a week of peacock fishing in the dry season of 1965.

My first catch of the trip was a caribe, *better known in the States by its Portuguese name,* piranha. *Overly excited, I paused to set up this photo, not realizing that I would soon grow very tired of catching and releasing (carefully) the ubiquitous saw-toothed pests.*

There are several species of peacock bass. Venezuelans call the largest variety Cebu *because of the hump on head of breeding males (Cebu is the Spanish name of the Brahma bull). The fish displayed here by Bill Morris is only a youngster, not yet a bull.*

Here I'm taking a close look at another and smaller species of pavon *that Venezuelan anglers called* mariposa, *meaning butterfly. Not being a soothsayer, I had no idea this species would be the one finally established in South Florida more than 20 years later.*

Carlos Galavis shows some hefty Cebu *peacocks he caught one morning in only the first hour of fishing. Every day we would travel by dugout canoe to different* caños, *which are creeks cut off from the river in dry season. In effect, each* caño *is an elongated lake with its own population of fish.*

A leaping peacock looks much like a snook. Indeed, we found them to be closer to snook than to largemouth bass in their striking and fighting qualities. One glaring difference, however, is that peacock bass allow the angler to sleep late. They simply refuse to bite at dusk or dawn, or at night

The saber-toothed fellow is a payara, *a tarpon-like jumper that can grow to nearly 50 pounds. Of the three "species" of peacock shown at right, the three biggest are* Cebus. *The little one is the butterfly peacock now well settled in South Florida.*

The fish on this stringer weighed 16-19 pounds. We caught others in this same range but none bigger. Carlos was disappointed that the 20-pounders eluded us. During his near-lifetime of fishing in that area he had caught several peacocks over 30 pounds and many that topped 20.

MORE POINTS SOUTH

Chapter 6

One morning in the spring of 1958, I was casting in the Rio San Juan near the remote village of San Carlos, Nicaragua. My guide was a young man named Cabo Enriquez, who was not really a guide at all, because guides had never before been needed in San Carlos. I was, in fact, the first foreign sportsman he had ever met, let alone been asked to take fishing.

Finally, Cabo got up the nerve to ask, "Don't you have fish in Miami?"

Being a truthful sort I had to admit that, yes, we did have fish in Miami, lots of fish, as a matter of fact. Cabo had suspected as much, so he blurted out the question that was really burning him:

"If you have fish where you come from, why do you travel so far to go fishing?"

My limited fluency in Spanish could not handle a philosophical discussion, so I merely shrugged and feebly replied, "To try different places."

During the Golden Age, I was by no means alone in my eagerness to explore new waters. Anglers from everywhere kept flocking to new angling destinations in the tropics as fast as they were being built, and that was pretty darned fast. Who really needed to ask why? Any ardent angler will tell you that the fish are always hungrier right over the horizon.

Maybe the bonefish in British Honduras (later Belize) weren't as big as those in the Florida Keys, but where else could an angler stand in one spot and rack up 72 bonefish releases in a day? Miamian Terry Wood—the wife of Gar Wood Jr.—did just that in 1962.

And maybe there really weren't more black marlin at Piñas Bay, Panama, than there were blue marlin in all the waters of Florida, but where in Florida—or anywhere in the world, for that matter—might an angler catch five big marlin of any species in a single day, as Helen Robinson did at Piñas in 1963?

And speaking of black marlin, maybe Panama had indeed produced hookups with a 1000-pounder or two, but during the 1950s black marlin weighing that much and more were being taken with unbelievable regularity at Cabo Blanco, Peru.

There just didn't seem to be any limit to the incredible fish tales flowing forth from tropical climes.

Some of the earliest and wildest reports in the early post-war period came out of Cuba, and the subjects of those stories were not the marlin that had so captivated Ernest Hemingway in pre-war days, but hordes of bonefish that were being taken at the Isle of Pines, and also—of all things—huge largemouth bass that had only recently been stocked in Cuba but were already going gangbusters in both number and size. It was a widely held belief in stateside bassing circles that the world record of 22 pounds, 4 ounces, was about to be not merely broken, but crushed. It never did happen, of course, but that record actually got pushed hard on several occasions.

Joe Brooks, the leading outdoor writer of that period, had been hired by the Batista government to publicize Cuban bass fishing, and he did it by sending down a virtual parade of American writers. Just before my name reached the top of Joe's invitation list, however, Batista was overthrown in 1959 by Fidel Castro, who thus deprived me of my slim chance to catch the record bass. Worse, he deprived Joe of his lucrative public relations account. Far worse, he came close to depriving Vic Barothy of a thriving bonefishing business. Fortunately, however, Vic had seen the writing on the wall and narrowly managed to sneak his boats and gear off the Isle of Pines and over to friendly British Honduras.

I might not have been able make Cuba anyway, for during my first year as fishing editor of the *Miami Herald,* my "duties" took me to a couple of more remote locales — first to Nicaragua and then a few months later to that world-famous hangout of monster marlin, Cabo Blanco. Although I found the fishing at both those locations fast and enthralling, in neither case did my enthusiasm result from the kinds of fishing advertised.

San Carlos, located at the far south end of 100-mile-long Lake Nicaragua, was trumpeted as a tarpon spot, but I ignored the tarpon in favor of sampling a variety of native freshwater species that were unfamiliar to me at the time.

As for Cabo Blanco, I never intended to hassle any thousand-pound marlin anyway. I simply used a women's international tournament as an excuse for making the trip. True, I diligently covered the tournament, but my ulterior motive was to sample Cabo Blanco's surf fishing, which angler-author Kip Farrington had told me was the best in the world. As usual, Kip proved to be the ultimate saltwater authority. I have since fished from many very productive beaches, but never one that another to equal the one at Cabo Blanco.

British Honduras (Now Belize)

In a backward sort of way, Fidel Castro was a key figure in the early development of British Honduras as an outstanding—no, make that spectacular—destination for sports fishermen. After Castro came to power in 1959, many private business owners in Cuba fled from nationalization with little more than the shirts on their backs, but Vic Barothy got out with the three houseboats—actually live-aboard cruisers--that had been the core of a highly successful fishing operation he had been running on the Isle of Pines.

When Barothy opened his new operation on the Belize River in British Honduras, he had something more to build the business on than just his houseboats. He brought with him a large and loyal pool of potential clients, built up over his many years of similar operations in the Florida Keys and on the Isle of Pines. Most importantly, he had scouted well, and had chosen a location that provided upriver access to a network of rivers, canals and inland bays loaded with such delights as snook and big cubera snapper. But the downriver route from camp led to fishing grounds that were even more compelling-- a vast and virtually untouched array of mangrove keys, flats, basins and channels reminiscent of the Florida Keys.

I first visited British Honduras in 1963 with George Robey, who, as manager of the Metropolitan Miami Fishing Tournament, was both a close associate and a frequent fishing partner. We had only three days to spend so did not embark on one of the trademark Barothy houseboat trips. Instead, we fished one day in nearby rivers and then took a ride out to Vic's as yet unopened new lodge in the Turneffe Islands, where we spent one night and fished one day for bonefish at the edge of the ocean, 25 miles from Vic's base camp on the mainland.

Had I thought to bring along a crystal ball I might have foreseen that in coming years I would visit Turneffe Island Lodge four times under three different owners, and would eventually count eight trips to British Honduras, where I fished more often than n any other foreign country except, of course, the Bahamas, which I considered part of my regular beat.

A family houseboat vacation brought me back to Barothy's river lodge in the summer of 1965, but that was my final visit there under his ownership. Failing health had caused him to sell his interests to Keller Caribbean Sports by the time my family returned for another houseboat trip with owner Fred Keller in 1970.

Lodges are still going strong on the Belize River and the Turneffe Islands. And, building on Vic Barothy's foundation, numerous other fishing resorts have sprung up over the years to blanket nearly the entire coast, from the Mexican border on the north to the Honduran border on the south-- as well as on the Ambergris Keys.

My last visit to British Honduras was in 1978, when Cheryl and I accompanied Karl and Sheila Wickstrom to Turneffe Island lodge.

I never did fish in Belize. All my fishing took place in British Honduras--long before the former colony became an independent country in 1987.

Pinas Bay, Where Marlin Play

It's a safe bet that the Pacific waters of Panama have produced more black marlin—thousands upon thousands of them—than any other place on the planet. It's also a pretty safe bet that at least three-fourths of those marlin have been taken within a two-mile radius of the Piñas reef (also known as the Zane Grey reef), a seamount located two miles offshore of Piñas Bay in the province of Darien.

Back in the 1950s, only a handful of adventurous and well-heeled anglers were fishing that area, and they did it by means of long-range cruises from the Canal Zone. One of those anglers was an oil and trucking magnate from Dallas named Ray Smith, who was so taken by the area that he proceeded to carve out a first-rate fishing lodge and marina on the shore s of Piñas Bay.

Before he officially opened his *Club de Pesca de Panama* in 1963, Smith recruited a group of outdoor writers and noted big-game anglers to "explore" the fishing prospects around his new resort. As outdoor editor of the *Miami Herald*, I was one of the anointed writers, along with Tom McNally of the *Chicago Tribune*, Paul Kalman of the *New Orleans Times-Picayune*, and Jennings Culley of the *Richmond News-Leader*. The chosen sportsmen were Miamians Gar Wood Jr., Jack Christianson and John Raulerson, plus Chilo Bird of San Juan, Puerto Rico.

Of course, those aforementioned long-range boats had been exploring the area for quite a few years but, nevertheless, all of us recruits diligently pursued the task that Ray Smith had assigned us, paying no heed to the obvious fact that we had been summoned far more for the purpose of exploitation than for exploration.

Tom McNally and I spent most of our four days casting with light tackle, while all others in our party chose to chase after marlin and sailfish. On our last afternoon I yielded to the temptation myself, and in not much more than an hour of trolling caught my first black marlin, a 246-pounder.

I did not return to Piñas Bay until after the Golden Age, 31 years later, this time with Biff Lampton, who had succeeded me as editor of *Florida Sportsman*. The name of the place had changed and so had the owners, but the boats were the same familiar 31-foot Bertrams, although re-worked and re-powered.

Ray Smith died in 1968, after which the Club de Pesca became Tropic Star Lodge. Conway Kittredge of Orlando purchased the club in 1976, and when Biff and I went there in 1994 it was under the management of daughter Terry and her husband Mike Andrews.

Southeastern Mexico

All the fishing I managed to do in Mexico got done in the states of Campeche, Yucatan, and Quintana Roo — the areas closest to Florida.

It started early in 1960 when George Robey and I traveled to a remote fishing camp on the western shore of the Yucatan peninsula called El Tarpon Tropical. There we tussled many a tarpon in the deep water of the Laguna de Terminos, but were far more enraptured by big snook that lurked in the surf a short stroll from our cabin.

Hal Hassey, an owner of El Tarpon Tropical, also took us by outboard far north of camp along the Yucatan coast and showed us schools of silvery baitfish, each school being battered by pods of medium-size tarpon. While jumping tarpon almost to the point of boredom, we began to experiment with different retrieve depths and discovered that speckled trout and snook were also feeding on those baitfish. Our enthusiasm renewed, we began trying to pick the kind of fish to hook next. If we retrieved a 52 Mirrolure near the surface it would be slugged by a tarpon. If we allowed that same lure to sink for a few seconds we usually could evade the tarpon and catch a trout. Best of all, we found that a heavier model of Mirrolure, or a bucktail jig, would usually sink quickly enough to clear both the tarpon and the trout and reach a gang of snook that was waiting patiently on the bottom for casualties to drift down to them from the surface.

With more time and fuel we could have continued northward to the tip of the Yucatan peninsula and then eastward to Cancun. But we would not have been impressed. Not until 10 or 15 years later would Cancun begin undergoing the rapid development that has led to its present status as the jewel of the "Mexican Riviera."

Before there was Cancun, however, (in terms of angling, I mean), there was Cozumel Island with its famous hordes of sailfish. And southwest of Cozumel on the mainland shore was Pez Maya, a leading light-tackle destination. And farther south yet, Ascension Bay offered an incredible inland network of flats and shallow bays, all inhabited, as one might guess, by additional swarms of permit and bones.

I loved them every one, but the picture has changed down that way. Although Cozumel can still brag about its sailfish, its primary fishing grounds are held in common with Cancun, and that's where the biggest fleets of offshore boats tie up these days. Angling still thrives at Ascension Bay but Pez Maya ceased operation in 1994, after which its holdings were purchased by the Nature Conservancy to become a vital piece of the Sian Ka'an Biosphere Reserve.

Just in time, too. By then, the Mexican Riviera had sprawled nearly 100 miles southward from Cancun all the way to Tulum, only a dozen or so miles north of Pez Maya.

Casting in Costa Rica

Few Latin America countries can boast of such angling diversity or so many first-rate fishing facilities as Costa Rica. All during the Golden Age, they kept springing up like weeds on both the Pacific and Caribbean coasts. And finally, as if meaning to cover all bases, by the end of the 1970s the country had even added some highly publicized bass-fishing to its offerings.

To be honest, that bass in Costa Rica is not the *largemouth* bass, but the *rainbow* bass. And to be painfully honest, the rainbow bass isn't a bass at all. Like the peacock--another faux bass that South Floridians have come to know and love—the rainbow bass is a cichlid. Costa Ricans avoid such confusion simply by using its Spanish name, *guapote*.

As interesting a fish as the guapote may be, however, it must remain only a minor player in the Costa Rican fishing league. It could hardly be otherwise, considering that the country's Caribbean waters have long been a leading destination for anglers seeking tarpon and snook, while its Pacific coast attracts legions of sportsmen eager to battle sailfish-- and a limitless menu of other gamesters too-- with trolling gear, spinning tackle, or flyrods.

In 1966 I joined a group that included George Hommell Jr., Ted Williams, Bill Barnes, and John Underwood on a trip to Parismina Tarpon Rancho—the first sportfishing facility on the Caribbean Coast. The camp, developed by Carlos Barrantes of San Jose, was not yet open to the public. As happened several other times during the Golden Age, I was called upon to help "test the waters" at a newly built facility, and I did my job without complaint.

Parismina proved a rousing success and in 1978 was to produce the all-tackle world record snook—53 lbs., 10 oz. Barrantes, a well-known sportsman and fishing tackle dealer in Costa Rica's capital city, went on to develop other tarpon lodges at Tortuguera and Casa Mar. Bill Barnes, a member of our exploratory group at Parismina, later became the longtime manager and eventual owner of the Casa Mar facility.

In 1971, during Easter vacation my 16-year-old son David accompanied me to a remote camp in the southwestern part of Costa Rica called Rancho Estero Azul. The lodge was located on the Sierpe River and we reached it by flying from San Jose to Palmar Sur and then taking an hour-long car ride through vast banana plantations. I had been lured there by tales of potential record-size snook, only to be told by owner Jerry Thornhill that access to the prime snook area had been cut off by a huge floe of hyacinths. We had to "settle" for red-hot action in the river on corbina, and fast jigging around outside islands for snapper, grouper, and jack.

My Tropical Fishing Photo Album

Perhaps because he knew English, a courtly gentleman named Abraham Downs was appointed greeter when J.W. Boettner and I arrived in San Carlos, Nicaragua. Noticing that we had "small tacklings," Abraham thought we might try fishing from shore, although he had doubts about our artificial lures. "Around here," he told us, "nobody have ever use pagan baits."

Abraham led us to the local "laundry" on the shore of Lake Nicaragua, where our "pagan baits" — small spoons — quickly drummed up action on silvery fish called machaca (lower left). Their high-jumping antics startled the washerwomen but did not really frighten them. They had learned to stay alert for a real threat — the infamous and dangerous bull sharks of Lake Nicaragua.

Doc Boettner of Fort Lauderdale caught the fish that Abraham Downs is holding. This trip, in 1958, marked my first meeting with the machaca, which would become familiar to me in many fresh waters of Central America.

These are jaguar guapotes, a somewhat smaller species than the related "rainbow bass." They weighed from less than a pound to slightly under 3 pounds, and they seemed to be the most aggressive of the different fish I caught in the San Juan River under the guidance of Cabo Enriquez, who was amazed that I had traveled so far just to go fishing.

The reason I'm showing off a mere croaker — in Spanish, roncador *— is because the ones in the San Juan River thought they were snook, striking surface plugs greedily.*

I journeyed to Cabo Blanco, Peru in January of 1969 to cover a women's marlin tournament. Kip Farrington had advised me to bring surf tackle and, since Kip was a leading saltwater fishing authority, I heeded his advice. My first before-breakfast catch was five corbina and two sierra mackerel. A kitchen boy came down to get the fish, so I had him snap this picture.

I enlisted Tom Turner of Winter Park to help battle those surf fish. He was on hand to cheer his wife Ellen, who was competing in the marlin tourney. For four days, Tom and I fished the surf mornings and evenings, riding as observers on the marlin boats in between.

This rock became our photo studio. The beach in front of the Cabo Blanco Fishing Club was about a mile long, with rocky points at either end. We caught mackerel and a few corbina all along the beach, but found our hottest action at the points.

Tom lands a sierra mackerel, a fish that to an angler's eye is identical to the Atlantic Spanish mackerel except for its much larger average size. Every sierra we caught ran literally true to the old fisherman's boast, "as long as your leg."

The club chef begged us to bring in all our fish, so Tom and I would string them up, using doubled 60-pound leader material, and drag them back. Here, Tom is about to drop our stringer in front of the club. Muscular members of the staff would be sent to carry the fish up the hill to the kitchen. Most of then ended up as seviche.

We found snook around the points, too. They ran about the same length as the corbinas, but were heavier – up to about 10 pounds. A few corbina pushed eight; most ran five or six.

Here I am hard at work — covering the marlin tournament between surf-fishing jaunts. Tough job I had, riding on a boat, taking notes, and helping the crew watch for fins. They never trolled blindly for marlin at Cabo Blanco. The fish were always spotted at the surface and individually baited.

The women fished hard and caught several smaller striped marlin, but could find only one black the entire week. Fortunately, I happened to be aboard when Ellen Turner — wife of my surf-fishing buddy — hooked up. Her catch became the high point of my newspaper coverage.

A fish this size would have drawn admiring gasps from onlookers if seen hanging almost any place except Cabo Blanco, where half-ton blacks were then roaming. Anyway, Ellen Turner's 442-pounder earned cheers from fellow contestants-- along with sighs of relief at escaping a black marlin shutout.

The driveway from the beach "highway" to the Cabo Blanco Club in Peru was lined with the tails of black marlin. By the time of my trip in January, 1959, 38 marlin weighing at least a half-ton had been put on the scale, including Alfred Glassell's 1560-pound all-tackle world record that still stands today.

This is Vic Barothy's lodge on the Belize River in 1963, about three years after its developer was forced to flee from the Isle of Pines, Cuba.

Vic Barothy doesn't look too impressed by the snook George Robey is lifting — or by the dozen more that George and I caught one morning out of Barothy's base camp. He'd seen a few before.

Barothy completed his Turneffe Island lodge in 1963. The Turneffe Islands offer many miles of bonefishing flats, creek fishing, and reef fishing. Over the years, I visited the lodge under three different owners.

Phillip Goff shepherds the invading Dunaway clan to the Barothy Lodge in 1965. That's Mari (15) on the dock, Dan (12) clinging to the suitcase, and David (10) in the bow. Wearing dark glasses is Cheryl (age withheld to protect the author). Next day we boarded the houseboat Vicki *for a week of roaming and fishing. On their first outing, both Dan and Cheryl got their first of many bonefish (below).*

The first tarpon that fell to the younger set — and the boys could scarcely believe it — was caught by Mari, who normally preferred sunning or reading over fishing. Skipper and chief guide John Ely led her to it.

Dan caught up with his sister when he bested the estimated 30-pound tarpon shown below. Arthur Villanueva was his guide.

David scored his first tarpon and first bonefish on the same day. They were not giants but neither was David, and so they look pretty big in the picture. I think he was prouder of his jack (R, which really was big.

Yes, tarpon and bonefish got to be old hat after a while, so Dan beamed when he pulled this 12-pound cubera snapper out of a creek near Turneffe Island Lodge. Capt. John took us over a lot of fishing grounds — as far as Ambergris Cay to the north and the Turneffes to the south.

We fast-forward to 1970 and our second family trip to British Honduras. Having already taken care of the bonefish and tarpon, Cheryl turned her full attention to looking for collectible bottles.

Here are a few bottles Cheryl tracked down on small islands in the Turneffe group. Phillip Goff dropped her off at an island he thought promising, and we picked her up at the end of our half-day of fishing.

Young bonefish were always easier to find in the Turneffe Islands than old bottles. The bones averaged a bit bigger there than they did closer to the mainland. On day I caught an 8-pounder. This isn't it.

Same pose, different anglers. At right, Dan connects with a bonefish on fly in the Turneffe Islands in 1970...

...And George Hommell Jr. does likewise on an exploratory 1975 trip to Ambergris Cay.

On my last visit to Turneffe Island Lodge, in 1978, I deep-jigged the nearby dropoff to take this 39-pound black grouper. It was my largest on a jig, but would have been no rare feat in the Keys during the heyday of light-line jigging in the 1960s.

A fleet of nine new 31-foot Bertram's lined up for the opening of Club de Pesca de Panama in 1963. Here, one of them is about to land a sailfish.

A black marlin jumps not far offshore of the mountainous jungle surrounding Piñas Bay. The black is the only marlin that sports long and rigid pectoral fins.

While most marlin caught at Piñas are now released, they were highly prized as food during the fifties and sixties and were generally brought in and carved up.

I have seldom seen dolphin as plentiful or of such big average size as the ones Tom McNally and I caught during that trip. They were everywhere, from the Piñas reef all the way to shore, where we caught them while casting against sheer rock cliffs. This cow I'm proudly lifting weighed 20 pounds.

I needed help hoisting this bull dolphin, which weighed 26 pounds. As I recall – and probably with no more exaggeration now than then – we didn't get a single dolphin under 12 pounds, and quite a few topped 20. On the other hand, we never ran across any real giants either.

John Raulerson was surprised when a 65-pound broomtail grouper swallowed his marlin bait over the Piñas reef. Here, with help, John hoists it high for my photo.

155

Tom McNally of the Chicago Tribune *leads a dolphin to boatside. Tom and I met on this trip and over the years remained good friends., Tom's son, Bob McNally of Jacksonville, now is a popular outdoor writer.*

Ho-hum, another big dolphin. Except for a few small tunas and three Almaco jacks, we caught nothing else with our casting tackle. We did get some excitement, though, when Tom lost a fly line and most of his backing in the area of the reef. It could have been one of those big broomtail groupers.

I caught my black marlin on the final half-day of fishing at Piñas. Most others in our "exploratory" party scored at least a couple of marlin and their total ran close to 20. It dawned on me that last day that I shouldn't pass up this golden chance to troll for a black myself.

At El Tarpon Tropical in Yucatan, Mexico, I caught three nice snook from the gentle beach in front of the lodge before breakfast. The fish were prowling a slough that paralleled the beach no more than 30 feet from dry sand. Owner Hal Hassey's tarpon gaff was a bit of overkill.

The three snook I caught that first morning weighed 15, 15, and 18 pounds. George Robey slept in long enough to miss the action but arose just in time to take pictures.

George Robey got up early the second morning and caught the 20-pounder in the foreground. I got two others. All hit yellow jigs.

Morning No. 3 at the Yucatan fishing lodge brought the first snook I ever caught on fly – and to this day it remains my biggest at 24 pounds. No great casting skill was required--only patience. I easily achieve the required distance of 50 feet or so, and kept at it until I finally got my one and only strike.

This shot of the great snook flyfisherman was taken after the fact. George had been fighting a snook of his own 100 yards away while I was struggling with mine. Afterwards, he stood by while I threw the streamer fly for a half-hour longer without another hit.

Nearly 10 years after El Tarpon Tropical – and on almost a straight line across Yucatan – this 15-pound permit was waiting for me near Pez Maya fishing resort, where bonefish and permit were small but plentiful.

The Caribbean beach in front of Pez Maya offered bigger fish. On this 1974 outing to the beach, Billy Pate, Bill Barnes and I landed two bonefish, a snook, several big jacks, and my estimated 25-pound permit, shown.

Al Pflueger and I conducted a couple of our fishing schools at Pez Maya in 1975. Al showed the students how it's done by landing this 20-pound cubera snapper from the inlet near our cabin. It took a hundred or more casts to do it. Few anglers have ever matched Pflueger in all-around skills, and none in perseverance.

Mako, then an independent boat company, held a writers' tournament at Cozumel in 1977. All the Mako boats, private and factory-owned alike, were shipped to the island by freighter. Here a sailfish gets released.

That's a 10-inch strip of pork rind on the bill of the sailfish. Harlan Franklin was fishing it behind a heavy trolling sinker in hopes of bagging a big grouper, but the Cozumel sails were so hungry they refused to leave any bait or lure unmolested.

Harlan Franklin gaffs a 50-pound wahoo. It was the only fish we caught while searching for a charted seamount 12 miles north of Cozumel Island. Harlan's 25-footer was one of the Makos shipped down for the tournament. On its return trip, the freighter and the little boats it carried were impounded in Cuba. After a suspenseful wait, all were restored to their owners.

SOME BOATS I'VE LOVED

Chapter 7

To an angler keeping his boat fed with gas, the Golden Age was almost literally golden. At many service stations in 1960 you could fill a 12-gallon tank for four dollars or so. Now, at the end of 2010, 12 gallons of gas costs something like 30 or 35 bucks. And that's at a roadside pump, not a marina.

"DUH," you say. "But don't we make much more money today?" Indeed we do. A median-income family makes eight times as much as in 1960. Gas costs 16 times as much. So let's just forget it and get back to some happier nostalgia.

In 1958, at a time when the majority of small fishing boats were still being built of plywood, I took delivery of my first consignment boat--a 14-foot FiberCraft. The company's name proudly denoted that all its vessels were made of a miracle material called fiberglass. Notice I did not say "space-age" material. Fiberglass had been appearing in fishing rods and a few privately made boats since the late 1940s, whereas the space age did not begin until the USSR launched its Sputnik satellite in 1957.

Neither that little FiberCraft nor any other boat at the time was being marketed as a "bonefish skiff." The designation was my own. I called it that because it sported a raised casting deck as an integral part of its molded cap. Nothing else suggested that it was particularly well suited to the fine art of bonefishing. It did have a mostly flat bottom behind a "V" bow, but that was the basic hull design of all fishing skiffs in that day and age.

To complete my "bonefish" boat I added the only two specialized accessories I could think of—a pushpole made from a wooden closet dowel and a handle extension for the 18-horse Evinrude that powered it. The extension allowed me to stand amidships while running in smooth water. Any sort of rough water was to be avoided whenever possible, which was virtually never. It seemed that every targeted fishing area was located on the far side of an open bay or basin, and that every fishing day brought with it a chop that was at least high enough—a foot, say—to rearrange all my gear and rattle all my bones.

Even though I loved as much of that little boat as I could stand, I was very happy a couple of years later when FiberCraft took it back and replaced it with a "real" bonefish boat—that is, a boat so labeled by the factory itself. Though only a foot longer, the new one was wider and—blessedly—considerably heavier with its 30-horse motor, integral 12-gallon gas tank, side steering console, and raised decks fore and aft. Such amenities were old hat to skiff guides in the Keys, but their boats were either built to order by local craftsmen, or else fitted or modified by the guides themselves. I'm pretty sure that 15 foot FiberCraft—a cut-down runabout hull with a reworked interior--was the very first boat ever promoted as a "bonefish skiff" by any factory.

Others who had that model were Capt. Bill Curtis and Capt. Stu Apte, two of the most highly publicized guides of the time. I fished frequently with both of them and I liked their FiberCrafts better than my own. That's because their boats were equipped with accessories mine lacked—eagle eyes and enthusiastic polers.

Those two FiberCrafts served me faithfully for a couple of years, but only in protected waters. And then, beginning in 1960 with a 15-foot Boston Whaler, I insisted that all the boats I used be willing to go anywhere from the Gulf Stream to the shallow flats. At one end or the other of those extremes, the various craft would show their displeasure by drenching me with salt spray or stranding me on a sandbar. Regardless, I still made them take me wherever I wanted to fish.

I agree that there is no such thing as a perfect boat, but in the early 1980s I finally did find the perfect one for me. It was a 16 1/2 -foot Hoog, rigged in flats-boat fashion and powered by a 90-horse Yamaha—and it was not a short-term consignment; I actually owned it! Its hull was a little too deep in the vee for easy poling in less than a foot of water, but that slight disadvantage was offset by the softest and driest rough-water ride I've ever experienced in any small boat. I got the Hoog in 1986 and kept it 20 years, re-powering after 18 years with another Yamaha 90.

In the end, I wore out before my Hoog did. It was performing as well as ever when I sold it in 2005. (Sorry. New Hoogs have not been built in years.)

Some Boats I've Loved
Photo Album

That's Jim Martenhoff, longtime boating editor of the Miami Herald, *at the wheel of my 15-foot FiberCraft in the fall of 1959. We often covered both boating and fishing angles of various outdoor stories. This time we were reporting on how to boat from Flamingo to Lostman's River, and how to fish the area if you ever got there.*

The 15-foot Boston Whaler, which came my way in 1960, was the first factory center console, and the first little boat that was truly safe for offshore operation. This shot, obviously, was not taken offshore. The angler with the snook is Ed Louys.

After the Whaler came this 18-foot Thunderbird, with its smooth-riding cathedral hull and a far roomier cockpit for the kids to roam around in. A cuddy under the forward deck provided refuge from rain.

Another view of the Thunderbird. I'm climbing back aboard after pinpointing a rock hole in Barnes Sound, Upper Keys, where snapper and grouper always hung out. Today, GPS does the job better but GPS doesn't cool you off.

I named all my boats "Poor Fish," but the 20-foot Scottie Craft I used through the heart of the 1960s, was the only one that displayed the name in print. Every inch of that Scottie was fishing space, and I took this boat offshore more than any of my others Above, Bob Lewis flies a kite off Key Largo for grouper – yes, grouper! – while Bill Barnes watches the baits.

I was happy to get several anglers their first sailfish by means of kite baits flown from the Scottie Craft. But I was happiest of all about this one – caught by my father, J. Dan Dunaway, near Careysfort light, North Key Largo

After the Scottie Craft came this Ouachita 14, a popular bass-boat of its day, but, like the other boats under my command, it was ordered to go everywhere – even offshore on calm days.

We used the Ouachita with its Electra Pal trolling motor more for shoreline snook fishing than anything else. Dan took this nice one on a surface plug from Lane Bay north of Flamingo.

I went bigger again at the end of the 1960s, to this 20-foot SeaCraft, one of many models of factory "fishing machines" — a term applied to center-console boats rigged out specifically for light-tackle angling. Here I'm taking John Bromfield to a spot near Marco.

The 17-foot Hoog remains my pet among all the boats I've ever had. I kept it for 20 years, and it was a true all-arounder. Above, Todd Richter is poling me across a Biscayne Bay bonefish flat in 1984. If you're wondering why the boat has no platform, see the next picture.

In preference to a poling platform on my Hoog, I chose to install pedestal sockets fore and aft to accommodate removable swivel seats — a sort of bass-boat touch that greatly increased the boat's comfort and convenience in shoreline fishing for snook and redfish, and yes, for bass too on less frequent occasions.

This may be the last photo of my beloved Hoog, taken at Steinhatchee in Florida's Big Bend in 2005. I sold it less than a year later. After 20 years, the only major changes were a second outboard motor, a third trolling motor, and a third pushpole.

NAME-DROPPING

Chapter 8

If there's anything staler than yesterday's news it has to be yesterday's television.

In 1969 and 1970 I co-hosted a pair of CBS specials entitled *Fisherman's World.* Each show consisted of several segments shot at various locations in this country and abroad. The shows enjoyed good ratings because, at that time, ABC's *American Sportsman* was the only fishing program appearing regularly on national television.

Today I am usually greeted by blank stares when I happen to mention the names of my co-host, John Bromfield, or any of the other prominent television stars who appeared as guest anglers on those shows. They were big names back then, too.

Bromfield was a Clark Gable look-alike who had starred in two hit TV series in succession—*Sheriff of Cochise* and *U.S. Marshall.* He had also performed in a few big-budget films and a raft of "B" movies.

Crooner John Gary, even at a time when rock and roll was already here to stay, sold millions of romantic records, had his own TV show, and hosted other popular shows.

Actor David Wayne had been the first Tony Award winner on Broadway and had appeared in many major movies, often as the second lead in films starring such

169

Hollywood legends as Spencer Tracy, Jack Lemmon, and Marilyn Monroe. He also had dozens of television roles.

And Garry Moore was undoubtedly the biggest TV name of his day. I don't know how he found the time to go on two of our fishing excursions because he was the host of three blockbuster hits on TV--two game shows: *I've Got a Secret* and *What's My Line?*, plus his *Garry Moore Show*, a variety program that served as a springboard to stardom for such talents as Carol Burnette, Jonathon Winters, Dorothy Loudon, and Don Knotts. (What? You say you don't remember *them* either? That's probably because you're younger than 50.)

Although I seldom garner any attention nowadays when I mention those erstwhile TV celebrities, I still see eyebrows lift whenever I drop the names of star athletes with whom I have shared fishing time both onscreen and off—Ted Williams, Boog Powell, Sammy Snead, Jack Nicklaus, Catfish Hunter. Like old soldiers who never die, old sports stars are immortal—not only because of their own splendid exploits, but because they are forever being compared to the athletic standouts of succeeding eras.

Tiger Woods? Well, at this writing he is struggling to regain momentum in his bids to overtake Sammy Snead in total tournament victories and Jack Nicklaus in major championships.

And what major league hitter has posted a .400 batting average since Ted Williams hit .406 in 1941? None, of course; not even Joe DiMaggio, Stan Musial, Barry Bonds, or Tony Gwynn, although a couple of them came close. But were the pitching staffs as strong? Was the ball the same? What might Ruth have accomplished had he laid off the beer? And what would some of the modern stars have done without steroids?

That's the kind of stuff that fans the flames of discourse wherever sports fans gather. The veterans are instantly recognized, their talents praised or debated, and their names spoken respectfully by fans who missed seeing them in person by several generations. On the other hand, we never seem to hear arguments about the relative maternal genius of TV mothers Donna Reed and Harriet Nelson, or the bedside manner of TV physicians Chad Everett and Robert Young.

But, actor or athlete, one thing that all the stars whose names I drop do have in common is that I remember every one of them well and fondly. There were no bad apples in the basket.

All the guests had their moments of angling glory, but Sam Snead's struggle with a blue marlin off Venezuela was the high point of the *Fisherman's World* programs. As big fish are wont to do, that marlin ignored our outrigger baits and instead sucked in a small ballyhoo that I had deployed in our wake in hopes of keeping smaller fish, such as dolphin and sailfish, away from our marlin rigs. And because of that backfiring strategy, Sam suddenly found himself hanging on to a spinning outfit from which 20-pound line was being ripped off as if by a jet plane.

After the marlin's first run, the spool of Snead's reel expanded and froze. In hopes of slacking the pressure long enough to do the job I had in mind, I instructed the skipper to back down rapidly while I ripped some line off an identical reel to make room on its spool. Then I tied the first line to the second. The knot held. Sam was in business again, but before we could resume normal breathing, the second spinning reel also froze up.

There followed another wild period of frantic backing to create slack once again. This time I tied the monofilament spinning line to the 50-pound braided Dacron line on a Fin-Nor trolling reel. So now Sammy at last was working with a reliable reel—but with three lines that were strung together by two hastily tied knots.

Somehow, everything held. Eventually, and with just enough light left to complete the filming, I sank the flying gaff into the 230-pound blue marlin. Under competitive angling rules, the catch would not have been "legal," but the travails under which it was accomplished added greatly to the filmed drama.

Anyway, Sam knew nothing and cared less about the competitive rules that prohibit tying two lines together or switching outfits. He laughed in delight as he inspected that huge fish lying on the deck, then he yanked off his signature straw fedora and plunked it down on my head.

Now I too had a trophy to crow about!

My Name-Dropping
Photo Album

Offshore trolling can be a slow business. While waiting for a marlin strike in Venezuela, Sam Snead dozed off. He woke to find a topless sunbather-- the boat owner's girlfriend-- lying on the engine box. Sam seems to be contemplating his next move. (Yes, the girl's chest is slightly retouched in the photo.)

Everyone aboard was laughing, Sam loudest of all. That's the lady's boyfriend sitting on the gunwale. (No, this incident did not make the TV show.)
A few hours later, all would be forgotten as Sam did battle with his first blue marlin.

At the dock where our private boat tied up in La Guaira, Sam Snead's 230-pound marlin is trussed and weighed. This is the only shot of the fish in my file. I was unable to take any action photos, of course, because I had been working the cockpit and the TV filming held priority.

John Bromfield stands handsomely on a balcony at Great Harbour Cay. I never understood why producer Fenton McHugh thought he needed a matinee idol to share hosting duties with me, but I was glad he did. Bromfield became a longtime friend.

John Gary enjoyed fame as a singer and also won respect as a diver. He held patents on two propulsion devices. The woman was a diver/model hired to brighten up an underwater segment at Andros Island, Bahamas.

That's John Gary impersonating the Creature from the Black Lagoon — as a jab at Bromfield, who confessed that in 1955 he had starred in Revenge of the Creature, one of several movies about the underwater menace.

David Wayne was not only a fine actor but also a skilled flycaster. Here he throws his fly to a tailing bonefish on the vast, sandy flats of Ambergris Cay in the Berry Islands, Bahamas.

He's on! Wayne's stance proved he was no stranger to the art of playing a long-running bonefish in skinny water. His catch was easily a 10-pounder, a praiseworthy fish on any bonefish flat.

Garry Moore landed this snook at Marco. A constant comedian, Garry devised a joke to play on producer Fenton McHugh. With the connivance of our crew, Garry and I filmed a segment that credited all our fishing success to the wondrous qualities of South Bend Tackle. Fenton had issued strict orders that the brand (for which I was a product advisor) was not to be billboarded. He was so upset when we played the tape that Garry had to 'fess up before Fenton collapsed.

John Bromfield and Sam Snead (in trademark straw hat) embark on a chilly South Carolina morning to chase striped bass in Lake Marion. This segment proved to be the most challenging of all. It was barely salvaged when Bromfield and Snead each bagged nice stripers on live baits the final day of shooting.

When I first fished with Jack Nicklaus at Great Harbour Cay in 1967, he had already won golf's Grand Slam, but was then in a mild slump that had some writers criticizing him as an underachiever. UnderWHAT? Jack won the U.S. Open that same year, then roared on toward an eventual record total of 18 major championships among 73 PGA titles. Sam Snead won more titles, 82, but only seven majors.

Jack eases a Bahamas bonefish toward the boat. I not only admired him for his angling and golfing prowess but also envied him for an entirely different ability: he enjoyed a cigarette or two whenever he went fishing, but was able to turn off the craving when he got back to shore. As for me, I had to keep huffing on land and sea until I turned 50.

Time to admire a nice catch. Of course Jack liked other kinds of fishing, but the few times we fished together in the Bahamas and the Florida Keys it was for bonefish. We once conducted a clinic together at Cheeca Lodge in Islamorada. Guess which one of us swung a golf club and which one a flyrod? I remember, but I'm not telling.

It's back to the old TV grind, but now the show is ABC's **American Sportsman**, *hosted by Curt Gowdy (in the checkered shirt). Capt. Bob Lewis is at the helm, looking for dolphin in the Tongue of the Ocean out of North Andros in 1968.*

Curt and I gang up on dolphin. I chose this location because schoolies were big and plentiful. How did I know? Because they were constantly stealing marlin baits from tournament anglers in the area.

This might have been Curt's best dolphin on fly during the show.. If not the biggest it certainly was the most brilliantly patterned. In life, dolphin change colors as quickly as a neon sign, but they go drab soon after dying.

This occasion was the 1975 Met Tournament opening-day banquet at Duck Key in the Florida Keys. The baseball luminaries with whom I'm sharing a laugh are Yankees manager Ralph Houk, Ted Williams, and Baltimore Orioles slugger Boog Powell.

Three legendary Keys guides listen as Ted Williams extols the wonders of Sears-Ted Williams spinning tackle. It's a pose, of course. All four knew each other well, and none dared question Ted's tackle. L-R: Cecil Keith Jr., Jimmie Albright, Ted, and Jack Brothers.

These happy anglers are New York Yankee greats Jim "Catfish" Hunter and Mel Stottlemyre. The famous pitchers caught their big sailfish on kite-flown baits one afternoon off Key Biscayne, following a morning of spring training in Fort Lauderdale. Hunter also caught an amberjack and released a second sailfish. I mated that day for Jim Hardin, himself a former major league pitcher turned fishing guide.

LOTSA LOBSTERS

Chapter 9

The magnificent coral reefs that extended from Southeast Florida through the Keys had not yet begun, in 1960, to show the effects of pollution, littering, anchor damage, and the many other perils that would cause grave problems in future years. Most of the shallow reef areas, whether large or mere patches, were vibrant and wore crowns of colorful fish to delight snorkelers.

Spiny lobsters seemed more plentiful too. Or was it just that fewer divers were gathering larger individual shares? Scientific opinion held that Florida's lobster population was, for all practical purposes, being harvested every year, and then replenished by Mother Nature before the next season rolled around. Regardless, it meant that many more lobsters were available for the taking.

Throughout the decade of the 1960s, my two grade-school sons and I spent every opening day of lobster season snorkeling in Barnes Sound, a shallow and easily accessible bay at the top of the Florida Keys, where the average depth was about eight feet. During none of those opening days did we ever see other divers, and most of the few vessels that did come into our view were plying the distant Intracoastal Waterway. Of course, our regular snorkeling grounds covered only one fairly small bay in the southeast corner of the sound, so there were might well have been a few other divers working beyond range of our vision, but there couldn't have been many, and we certainly didn't care.

Yes, there was a size limit back then but no official bag limit, although on opening day I personally imposed a cap of 50 lobsters, total, for the three of us. But that wasn't so much a bag limit, really, as a cutoff point. By the time we had captured that number, we were more than ready to leave the water and start nursing the various minor wounds administered to our bare arms and chests from antennas, spines and corals.

We didn't use nets and we hadn't even heard of "tickle sticks." We employed the simple tactic of reaching gloved hands into coral-crusted dens and working around the lobster's prickly antennas until we could grab hold of its head. After a twisting, tugging struggle that often lasted right up to the limit of one breath--and sometimes required a second or third dive after surfacing for a gulp of air-- we almost always managed to yank the delicacy from its den.

If we were to go out this year on opening day, whether to Barnes Sound or any other shallow and convenient area in the Keys, we would surely encounter a veritable armada of competitors, some of them possibly within a pebble toss of our own boat.

MY LOBSTER DIVING PHOTO ALBUM

When he waged this battle with a reluctant "bug," Dan was eight years old. David began going after them the following summer at age 7.

Dan bobs to the surface for more air—an indication that his intended prey was wedged tightly in its hole, or perhaps even hidden around a bend. We frequently had to probe elbow-deep, and occasionally even armpit deep, to dig out a reluctant lobster.

David proudly displays his first lobster, captured at the age of seven. The gardening gloves were swiped from his mother. They were the only gloves we could find that came close to fitting.

I score a double on spiny lobster. It was common to find more than one occupied hole in a single hump of coral; sometimes there would be three or four. Our Thunderbird boat in the background isn't as far away as the lens makes it seem.

Another year, another boat. Dan, now 10, hands over a catch to eight-year-old David, who stands in our second 15-foot Boston Whaler. We used the Thunderbird (previous photo) for two years in between Whalers.

Although nearly every one we encountered was of "keeper" size, the lobster in David's left hand was especially big. The spiny lobster can grow to several pounds but few of them in Florida's hallows — even during the Golden Age — got the chance to live so long.

Here we have all the lobsters four hands can display. Our access point was Gilbert's on U.S. 1 at Jewfish Creek. In Dan's expert opinion, the cook at Gilbert's Restaurant turned out the best cheeseburgers in Florida. I bring up the point only to explain Dan's expanding torso.

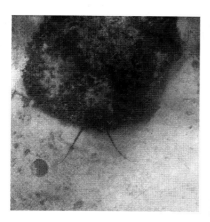 

Antennae protruding from under a sponge were the sure giveaway of a lobster's presence (L). The huge "bug" that David is holding at right was not caught in Barnes Sound, The boys found it lurking off the beach at Treasure Cay, Bahamas.

During our early years we always swam back to the boat to deposit each catch but finally we caught on to the convenience of suspending a net below an inner tube and pulling it behind us. This also allowed us to range father from the boat. "Diver Down" flags were not required by law in those days.

Traffic sometimes got heavy around our lobster-holding net. The grinning guest diver on the right is the boys' uncle, Frank Davis of Pompano Beach. This shot was taken in 1967 when the boys were 14 and 12.

David was away at boarding school when Capt. Jim Drummond invited Dan and me to go lobstering off Key Largo aboard his charter boat Drumbeat *in 1968. I have gained a couple of pounds in the years since somebody sneaked this shot while I was gearing up. Snorkeling or free-diving required only minimal equipment. I never developed an interest in scuba.*

Dan and I pose at the surface during our Drumbeat *outing. We seldom went lobstering on the outside in our own boats because out there we always got sidetracked by fishing.*

Dan, 15, shows off our day's catch at Drumbeat's *berth. I don't remember how many there were, and I can't count them in the picture. But it doesn't really matter because there was no bag limit in the sixties*

187

EPILOGUE:
A New Age

The passing of the Golden Age is not to be lamented but celebrated.

In the Golden Age we became fully aware of just how extensive and varied our fabulous sportfishing resources really are, and we learned many new ways to enhance our enjoyment of those diverse riches. So let's hear a loud hoorah for that long-gone period, while saving a louder hoorah for the New Age--the age we enjoy today.

While it's true that many kinds of fish are no longer as plentiful as they once were, it's equally true that Florida is now maintaining what once had seemed nearly impossible: a high level of top-quality angling for an ever-increasing population of resident and visiting sportsmen. Careful management, tight regulation, and constant vigilance by a conservation-minded public, have wrought the miracle.

We are fortunate that the Golden Age gave way to a period which began as difficult and painful yet in the end turned out to be the salvation of the state's fishing future. I look upon that period, which ran from the early 1980s well into the 1990s, as an age of enlightenment, a time when Florida's sportsmen—rallying behind the strong leadership of Karl Wickstrom and *Florida Sportsman* magazine, along with the Florida Conservation Association (now CCA of Florida) and a stout cadre of other far-seeing individuals and organizations--emulated the famous movie line *I'm mad as hell and I'm not going to take it any more,* and persevered until they managed to carve a remarkable degree of order out of what had become a chaos of governmental failures, commercial excesses, and, yes, poor management of recreational fishing as well.

My own golden years (which are definitely *not* to be confused with a Golden Age) began at just about the time the smoke was starting to settle a bit from those great conservation battles.

I now fish more for relaxation than adventure, and my usual targets are redfish and trout along the Big Bend coast. Those are the species that started my saltwater fishing in the first place and the pursuit of them is no less intriguing to me now than it was nearly three-fourths of a century ago. To be precise, it has been 75 years at this writing since I caught my first speckled trout at Live Oak Island in Wakulla County at the age of eight. It was a keeper, too. Of course, they all were back then!

As wonderful as trout and reds may be, however, I found that man—at least *this* man--cannot live by trout and reds alone. After the many years I put in chasing more muscular species, I find it difficult to stay away from them entirely, so in what have become my home waters, I might still hassle a few cobia and grouper from time to time, and even an occasional big tarpon (by surprise, not design). My regular launching spot is a ramp at the mouth of the Withlacoochee River near Yankeetown; however, Crystal River, Cedar Key, and Suwannee are all within easy driving distance for a one-day outing.

I still wander around Florida too. Since "retiring," (from regular office hours; not from writing, and certainly not from fishing), I have literally fished the far corners of the state—Pensacola, Jacksonville, and Key West—along with many chosen spots in between, most obviously the Stuart area, the home of outsize snook, humongous trout, and *Florida Sportsman* magazine.

Happily, my two sons Dan and David, who figure prominently in this volume, live within easy travel distance of my home in western Marion County, and daughter Mari is not that far away. She lives in Tallahassee, the very town in which she was born. The boys and I still fish together with fair frequency, usually out of Yankeetown but sometimes in fresh water. Dan and I used to go after redbreast bream in the Rainbow River, but since I now live on the Withlacoochee and can catch bream from my dock, we mostly reserve our fishing time for the salt. We do sometimes join David in fishing for speckled perch and other panfish on Orange and Lochloosa Lakes, which are waters David knows well, since he has lived between them for a long time and was a bass guide during the heyday of "hawg" fishing back in the 1970s.

And now I have another generation of anglers to fish with. Mari's daughter Victoria, like her grandpop, was a pre-schooler when she landed her first speckled trout on an outing with me and her dad, Johnnie Patronis, near Yankeetown. Now, at this writing, she is a recent graduate of Florida State—a third-generation Seminole, no less. David inherited two fine kids when he married, then he and Sheri added two more. My step-grands are Angela and Kenny, both now grown and gone from the nest but living close by. Grandkids Destiny, 12, and David, 10, are eager anglers and first-rate scallopers.

Destiny displayed a keen eye for fish early on. During a fishing and scalloping trip to Steinhatchee when she was seven, she maintained the family tradition by catching her first speckled trout. Although she had never seen one before, she had no doubt about its identity.

"That's a Dalmatian fish," she proclaimed.

ABOUT VIC DUNAWAY

One morning in the early spring of 1928, J. Dan Dunaway and Maggie Belle Harris Dunaway left their Southwest Florida home to go fishing on nearby Lake Trafford. They returned with the double brace of hefty largemouth bass shown above. Even in that distant time the fish were noteworthy for their size, but perhaps even more remarkable for the influence they apparently had on the unborn child who was along for the ride that fateful day. A few months later—on October 10, 1928—Vic Dunaway came into the world in Fort Myers, Lee County, Florida.

So it's true! Vic Dunaway was fishing before he was born!.

After graduating with a degree in journalism from Florida State University in 1950, Vic worked as sports editor for two daily newspapers before starting his full-time outdoor writing career with the *Miami Herald* in 1958. After more than 10 years as the Herald's outdoors editor, he became founding editor of *Florida Sportsman* magazine in 1969.

Although he retired from the desk in 1992, he continued to write regularly for *Florida Sportsman* while turning out a string of popular books on fishing and fish cookery.

One of his early books—*Vic Dunaway's Complete Book of Baits, Rigs and Tackle*—has for more than 40 years been considered a standard reference by fishermen at every level of experience, and is an all-time best seller.